MW00397222

Hindsight Joy

A Story of Removal and Redemption

Royce Brehm

Royce C. Brehm

Hindsight Joy

Hindsight Joy

Royce C. Brehm

The Introduction

A brand new believer in Christ should really be careful what scriptures to begin their discipleship with, right? A new believer that has lived a life of self-inflicted pain and suffering, addiction and loss could easily be expelled from the faith if they start with a scripture such as James 1:2, right?

Consider it pure joy when suffering? The new believer has spent his life suffering. How can this text be encouraging? How could this text be one that would help this new believer continue in the decision that he made to follow Christ? I mean, he made this decision for ease of life, for things to get "better", for his pain and suffering to end, right? It would be like buying a new food brand and being excited that it has benefits for health, and maybe even longevity. But then, the label says, "Be happy and smile when this product tears your stomach to pieces sending you in to violent nights of vomiting and diarrhea. Makes all the sense in the world, right?

All of this is untrue. But only IF this new believer thinks back to his former life and sees the importance of the things that he was rescued from when he surrendered to a Savior that loves him. All scripture is God-breathed and straight from Him. So, the text in James 1 is exactly where God wanted this new believer to start in his new walk with Christ. I am that new believer, and I see the joy in the things that I have been through. The joy of redemption through Jesus is remarkable in ALL cases, but in my case, it's personal and close. I am Royce Brehm, and I am redeemed by the blood of Jesus!

Chapter One

The Beginnings of Removal

My father, Roy, was a great man. He was a man who loved unconditionally. His life served to teach me and my two sisters, Jackie and Shara, to be content and to love each other through all the problems of the world. Through all of his problems that brought many struggles in our family as we grew up, he remained a great father. We never doubted his love for us and even today, we understand his struggles and we take his heart as an example of what love is.

Dad, or Pop as we all knew him, was born to a single mother. This part of his life was seldom talked about so my knowledge of the situation is limited. Pop was adopted by a German couple fifty-something years older than he. His grandparents were German immigrants who escaped the horrors of German oppression and settled in San Antonio, Texas as farmers. Ernest and Elise Brehm, known as Oma and Opa to us kids were terrific people. I remember many days and nights at their farmhouse on Walzem Road playing in the fields, on a tire swing and petting their German shepherd,

Shotzi and having to be really careful around Oma's antiques. Oma adored antiques. She was a friend of First Lady, "Lady-Bird" Johnson because of her love for these beautiful pieces. Opa was a rugged, hard working man who was active well into his later years on the farm.

My memories of my grandparents are vivid, pleasant. It still humors my sisters and me to talk about the days that Oma and Opa would argue, but would do so in German dialect in order to spare us children the worry of their differences. They called dad Butch and Oma took that an affectionate step further, Butchy. We rarely heard them refer to Pop as Roy; unless of course they were angry at him for something. Some of my favorite stories that Oma would tell were those of the shenanigans that Pop would get in to in his teenage years. Pop was really fond of "dune buggies" and "Baja" exhaust altered Volkswagen Beetles. Fast cars that would go off-road were his thing. One story that was a favorite of mine was when he ran from the police through open fields knowing that police cruisers in the 1960's couldn't catch up to him in his off-road buggy. Another was the time he was at a stop light that looked like the starting line of a drag strip. A street car with obvious muscle pulled up beside Pop in his Baja Beetle and wanted some speedy action. Pop knew that he would be dust when this race started so he turned to his delinquent creativity to be the winner. As the drivers looked each other in the eyes with the revving of the engines, dad popped the clutch as if he was taking off, and immediately stomped the brakes. The traffic light had not given the go signal, but the street car driver accelerated due to the flinch of the beetle and was "T-boned" in the intersection. Pop carried on with his ride with victorious arrogance.

Pop wasn't always a trouble maker. He was a hard working baseball player that traveled to many states to play. He was a left-handed centerfielder who was known in the area as one of the best. He was also a very very talented trumpet player which was actually how he ended up meeting the love of his life and his future wife, my mother, Martha Regina Moss. One day, on the steps of the band hall at Judson High School in Converse, Texas, Pop walked right up to my mom and kissed her as if they had been an item for months. The jagged-around-the-edges tough guy just kissed the military man's daughter. The bad boy and the beauty queen majorette just had a "moment". Mom was repulsed at this display of a "pick up" attempt. Little did she know it worked.

Momma was the good kid; the girl you would want your daughters to be like. She was born in Selma, Alabama to a career military man, Jack Harper Moss and the larger than life Sarah Mitchell Moss. They were my other grandparents. Nana (Sarah) was tough as nails. I was fortunate to have a great relationship with her throughout my years and we grew close as best friends. We bowled in leagues together, went fishing frequently and we loved to watch wrestling. During my bench-warming stints in baseball and football, she would be the loudest person in the stands, imploring, or demanding that the coach "put Roycie in!!!" She was an umpire or referee's worst nightmare. Her last healthy years before strokes took over were spent in the stands at Sewell-Thomas Stadium at the University of Alabama yelling at umpires and admiring players like Eddie Looper and Mike Tradawski. She was the baseball team's biggest fan. I do not have any memories of Pakka (Jack). He passed away when I was just a baby, but from what I know, he shared the tough persona of his wife despite his short frame. Nana was a lot taller than he was, but Pakka was a great home leader to Nana and their five children.

Mom had three brothers, Allen, Ike and Richard and one sister, Paula. Mom was sandwiched right in between the five in age. She affectionately known as "Sissy" and was the nurturing sister who helped parent the others as Pakka was usually busy at work or stationed somewhere other than home. Today, her nieces and nephews still call her Aunt Sissy. My mother's role as a stand-in parent growing up helped make her the greatest mother in the history of the world. No need went unmet and momma always made sure that our extra-circulars were in play. If my sisters had a beauty pageant and money was tight, she would do without. If they had a baton twirling competition, she made sure they were at practice and the uniforms were bought. In football and baseball season, she made sure I was where I needed to be and my games were attended. It seemed like she was always able to be in six places at one time. It was amazing to see her be a mother. In the midst of all the busyness of her children, she took unconditional love to the highest level. (More on that later).

After high school, my dad had decisions to make that every athlete in the world would love to have. Play baseball in college or play baseball for money. Pop was good enough to be drafted right after high school and gained the attention of all the major universities in Texas. Even in his highest time of notoriety and attention, he and momma stayed together. Pop knew that he would marry her from the first time they spoke on the steps of Judson's band hall. The future sure did look bright as it appeared that they would live a life of plenty as he played the game that he loved. When he was drafted to play professional baseball, it all looked like a reality. Momma had a couple of years left in high school and Pop could go and play baseball and have the money to make a great life for her after graduation and marriage.

The world was in turmoil at the time. The Vietnam War had been in full scale chaos for years. The United States needed more manpower and instituted the Draft in order to replenish the depleted troops. The war wasn't going without major protests by citizens, mainly those at universities and people in their early twenties. It wasn't a great time to be a soldier if you were looking for praise and admiration. Soon after Pop was drafted to play baseball, he was drafted into the United States Army, the first of many planned removals in the history of my family. What was God's plan in all of this? Pop's baseball talents probably wouldn't serve him very well in battle within the Vietnamese jungles.

I really do consider myself to be the luckiest brother in the world. As mentioned earlier, I have two sisters, Jackie; two years older than me, and Shara; almost four years younger. How could the only son and the middle child be the luckiest brother in the world? Those two were the best sisters in the world while we grew up. We were all really close. Our support of each other was the bond that made us so close. It took a lot for me to want to support them at baton twirling competitions that last all day and night and usually required they be there before 7 am. How absolutely boring for a boy to sit and watch baton twirling on his Saturday! Most competitions involved my mom and my sisters showing extra effort to set me up with one of their teammates. It was annoying at times but sometimes flattering that they wanted me to have a girlfriend and some of the candidates actually seemed interested.

Even worse than baton competitions were the beauty pageants that I was dragged to. I hated those things; and still do! A building full of already pretty girls who spent way too much money on dresses and hair and makeup only to make themselves look less appealing; in my eyes anyway. I prefer the beauty of a girl who wakes up and throws up a pony tail and takes little effort in changing the beauty that God already blessed her with. Anyway, beauty pageants were the norm around my house. Jackie took part in more of them than Shara did. I remember when we lived in Oklahoma City and Jackie won some sort of Miss Oklahoma pageant. She won a ton of prizes and the biggest was a small (but bulky in today's standards) COLOR television. You know the one, with 2 knobs, one that goes through channel 13 and has a "U" that you must keep it on in order for the lower knob to tune into channels 14-42. That TV ended up being the TV in my bedroom growing up. We didn't have cable in the bedrooms so the screws on the back of the TV were used for my homemade satellite dish. I took the plug of a small lamp that a friend gave me for Christmas and screwed one prong from the plug into the screw holes on the back of the TV and hooked the lamp to my bed's headboard. Believe it or not, it brought in three extra channels that I otherwise would not be able to get. The only problem now was not having a channel that didn't end its broadcast day with a Willie Nelson environmental commercial followed by the National Anthem at 11:00pm.

It may have seemed that my support and attendance at my sisters' competitions was forced on me, but I actually did love seeing them be good at what they were doing. And seeing them win a whole bunch was rewarding for me as their brother. They returned the favor in their support for me. I

7

played baseball and football and they were always there watching and cheering for me. Our bond continues to this day although it is really difficult to stay in touch with our busy lives and the fact that we live in three different corners of Alabama.

Chapter Two

The Family That Loves Each Other......

I had times in my life that I really hated the idea of having a daughter. Most of these thoughts were sparked by my sisters' dating lives. I was very protective of them, sometimes a little overprotective. With Jackie, Twinkle Toes as Pop called her, being older than me, it was hard to try and scare any boys away from her in an effort to keep her safe from what I knew was the corrupt, immoral mind of a teenage boy. My routine in this event was to try and do things to embarrass Jackie and run the guy off. I'd turn to "bodily functions" to achieve my goal; and I would just be so annoying that maybe the boy wouldn't want to return. Seldom did it work. Jackie was one of those girls that never was single, though she didn't "play the field" either. Each of her relationships was lengthy and lasted a long time. She basically dated the same boy all the way through high school. I liked him a lot. He was the quarterback of another local school and a fantastic baseball player. I just knew that they would end up getting married when they decided to attend Troy State University together. God had other plans for her.

Jackie graduated from Troy State University with a degree in Journalism and Public Relations. She married Todd Edmondson and he would've been my pick for her husband if I'd known him earlier. He is such a great guy and fantastic supporter of Jackie and their two daughters, Sarah Kate and Mary Elizabeth, who I call Pooh and Pooh Too. I have nicknames for everyone! Jackie is the Public Relations Director for Gadsden State Community College and Todd is some sort of Investment Banker and they live in Glencoe, just outside of Gadsden, Alabama. The most impressive aspect of their lives together is their love for charity. Jackie is a fundraising Phenom of sorts and has won numerous awards for her efforts in raising funds for a new Boys and Girls Club in Etowah County. She serves on several boards of different non-profit agencies and excels in helping these organizations function. It is incredible to see her work in this capacity.

Shara, or to Pop, Binky, never really had great taste in the boys she dated. Some were a little rough to say the least. I did all I could to scare most of them away but when I went to college, she was just entering high school, the prime time for dating. The fact that she had big, strong mean brother hours away didn't deter these guys from being around her. All I could do was call regularly and be really nosey in my questioning of her dating life. I loved my little sister! My protectiveness started immediately when she was born. I was always very concerned about her taste in boys and that she may end up with some loser that wouldn't take care of her the way that I felt she deserved. Scripture tells us not to throw our pearls to swine, and Binky was my pearl and these "Pigs" didn't deserve to have the pleasure of my sister's hand in marriage.

She really did ease my concerns when she met her husband, Terry Lingenfelter while they attended Montevallo University. This guy is the polar opposite of every boy she ever dated, and that was definitely a great thing. His only flaw is his fandom of the Pittsburgh Steelers. You'll understand why that bothered me down the line. Terry is a hard worker. He is a civilian engineer at Red Stone Arsenal in Huntsville. I have absolutely no idea what he does at work and I believe it's supposed to be that way. I just know he is good as gold to my pearl and I'm grateful for him. They have two kids, Emma, or Pooh-Trey, and Troy. These kids, like their cousins are super talented. Shara is the Administrator for a Pharmaceutical Company in Huntsville and doing really well for herself.

My mother is still the same loving, caring and supportive woman that I have always known. When we first moved to Alabama in 1984, mom went to school and completed a nursing degree all while raising three kids in a rough neighborhood in Northport, a city just outside Tuscaloosa. Dad was working for our uncle building cabinets and installing stadium seats and this job took him out of town quite often so mom's job of raising us was tough. She did great. Nana (Sarah) lived across the street and helped out but momma was all we needed. After she graduated, she went to work at DCH Regional Medical Center (Druid City Hospital as it was known then) where she stayed until she retired a few years ago. She worked the night shift for most of that time there. She was a great provider and it seemed like she preferred working while we were sleeping so that she could be around in the afternoons to be at all of our many events.

Today, momma lives in Irondale, Alabama with my step father, Terry or "Papa Chewy' to his grandkids where she spends most of her time working hard for the city while Terry serves as a City Councilman. She volunteers at the Senior Center and helps coordinate events for the city. With her fiery attitude and opinions, she also actively pushes for things that she knows will better the community she lives in while attending city council meetings and giving the mayor and other councilmembers a hard time about being politicians and not humans. She is a regular on nightly newscasts if there are any controversial decisions to be made for the city she loves. She cares that much about people. She is the foundation of the love that our family has for each other. I put her through a lot in my shenanigans and she loved me anyway and prayed for me often which worked as you will find out later. I couldn't mention our family without mentioning my step brother Kelly and my step sister Connie. When those two were added to the family, all five of us realized that we could've been siblings all our lives. We are fortunate to have these new additions!

My dad is such a big part of my story that I will save his description for later on.

Chapter Three

The Beginning of My First Love Affair

When I was born on July 8, 1976, some people would have thought that I would end up being a massive human being with my dad's athletic ability. I weighed in at a whopping 10 pounds and 14 ounces. Seemed that whatever my mom was eating, I was stealing all the nutrients and calories from her! The first thing most men say when seeing a baby that size for the first time is "That kid is going to be a big ol' football player". I am pretty sure my parents had extreme anxiety on how they would afford to pay for this huge child to eat. Looking to the future, it appeared that mom and dad had birthed a future football animal that may not require much work due to the size that God had apparently blessed me with.

None of that ended up being the case; except maybe the football animal part! By the time I had reached kindergarten I weighed only 25 pounds. I had only gained 14 pounds since birth and didn't grow much taller. I was a termite! I started school at Plaza Towers Elementary School in Moore, Oklahoma near Oklahoma City. My first school made worldwide headlines a couple years ago when tornadoes destroyed the school and the neighborhoods around it. At that time, elementary schools had athletics and my school had football!

We lived in a straight road neighborhood on Telephone Road, full of kids whose dads all worked in the Oil Fields. The company they all worked for had bright red vehicles and that straight street we lived on was lined perfectly with these bright red cars and trucks. There was always something to do on that street. I spent much of my time in backyards playing tackle football with the older kids. At the age of five, I was first introduced to being a "bad kid" from me always being around the older kids. I was small so I had to be tough! One afternoon, as we were resting from a tackle football game and eating popsicles in a front yard, the older kids dared me to yell some colorful expletives at the approaching newspaper delivery boy. In those days, newspapers were delivered on a bicycle, typically by a young boy trying to earn a little money. In my constant efforts to impress the older kids, I did what they dared me to do.

Now, the newspaper boy was older than the "friends" that I was hanging out with and I didn't realize that he was old enough to tell my parents exactly what I said. The expletive rhyme involved seven words and every word was not something I needed my dad to know that I said. Remember the red vehicles? I wrongfully used them to my advantage. To my shock, when the newspaper boy asked my "friends" where I lived, they sold me out and told him! I couldn't believe that they all pointed in the exact direction of my house and said almost in unison, "Down there where the red car is parked." My house was a pretty good distance down the straight road and on the left side of the road according to the direction that I took off running in. As I sprinted with my tiny legs in an attempt to beat the tattle tale to my house to act like I had been in my back yard all along, I came up with an evil plan to use all those red cars to my advantage.

All through my life, I have had a nemesis. Usually this is in the sports world. The guy that I heard squat more weight than me, the defensive lineman that had more sacks than I had the week before; things of that nature. Well my first nemesis was Jimbo. My disdain for this kid wasn't due to his athletic prowess, him beating me in any games at school or anything to do with sports; it was his hair. You see, I was blessed with bleach white curly hair. Jimbo had the popular "spike" haircut of the early 1980's. I was jealous because my curly hair simply wouldn't "spike". I despised him for this because he was the little girls' favorite and he was as arrogant as a five-year-old could be about his looks. But overall, Jimbo was a good kid; the problem with him was all my problem. Here is why this matters.

As I ran to beat the newspaper boy, the thought of "getting even" quickly sprung me into action! Jimbo's dad also drove one of those bright red vehicles and his family happened to live right across the street from us. So, instead of making a left and running into MY backyard, I made a right, straight into HIS backyard. I squatted down behind the porch after I defeated the newspaper boy, who was on a bike while I was on foot (a foreshadowing of my speed). He parked his bike in the driveway and walked up to the door. I assume the conversation with who he thought was my father, went something like, "Sir, your son just cussed me out down the street around all of his older friends a few minutes ago", and he likely didn't get the third of seven words out of his mouth before the front door slammed and Jimbo's father began calling loudly for Jimbo to come inside. I am not certain where on the street Jimbo was. At any given time, there would dozens of kids outside playing.

A few minutes later, the newspaper boy was gone and wasn't able to point out the potty mouth to Jimbo's dad when Jimbo got inside the house. The next thing I heard was Jimbo pleading that he was innocent and the next sound was that of leather slapping across the backend of Jimbo's Tough Skin Jeans. I was more than thrilled. Not only had I got Jimbo in trouble for doing something that I actually did, I also got to hear the punishment. Guilt was nowhere in my conscience; it was happiness. I can't remember how the next thing happened, but Pop ended up finding out what I did, the seven word rhyming expletive AND the part about me going in the wrong backyard and getting Jimbo falsely accused. I got double the punishment.

That neighborhood and my insistence on playing tackle football with older kids taught me how to be tough. There were times that I had to fight just to get home. I was born with a huge body, was living with a small body at the time, and I possessed a temper that couldn't be tamed, no matter the size of the person who was pushing my buttons enough to bring it out. I would fight anyone! But that neighborhood also made me LOVE football, my first love; other than my family of course. Moore, Oklahoma wasn't too far from Norman, where the University of Oklahoma was located. It was the early 1980's and the Sooners were the best football program in the country and Barry Switzer, the head coach was my hero. One day, I wanted to play for Coach Switzer and the Sooners.

When I found out that Plaza Towers Elementary had a football team, The Road Runners, I just had to play! Of course, momma and Pop had concerns. I was so small. But the concerns weren't for my safety, but how would they find football pants and pads small enough to fit me? The fact is, it was impossible. Back in those days, all football pants were white and you would have to use dye to make them another color and our pants were to be black. As I first put on my first pair of black dyed pants, the smallest size available, they went all the way down to the tops of my cleats. My knee pads protected my shins and ankles and my thigh pads covered the rest. That isn't typically how it is supposed to work. I didn't care, I was playing football.

When practice started, school was just starting too. I didn't know many of the kids on my team, just a couple from my street, particularly Kyle Holman, who was my best friend. We spent most of our time mimicking professional wrestlers and wrestling was mostly his thing. He wasn't near as small as I was but wasn't all that interested in football even close to the level that I was. On the first day of football practice, a car pulled up carrying the last of my new teammates to show up to practice. As the other kids showed up, I would look them up and down, sizing them up and determining how I would go about establishing my dominance on them so they would forget how little I was.

I wasn't really sure how to "size up" this last arriving teammate. I was having a hard time devising my plan to establish anything on this player.

Hindsight Joy

Nothing was crossing my mind like, 'he is tall so I will hit him in his knees, he's heavy so I will have to be quicker than he is', the typical thoughts that I had while sizing up the other 23 players. When the door opened, a fully padded football player ready for battle with the look of a killer stepped out. It was a girl; Angel. She had long blonde hair. She was bigger than most of us boys, not in an oversized offensive lineman sense, but a linebacker or a bruising running back. I could not believe that I was going to be playing football with a girl; one who was actually the only teammate that I couldn't figure out a plan of action against. It wasn't only from the fact that I was taught never to hit a girl; I figured if she knew what she was getting into, she was going to get hit; my problem was that I was terrified of her and so were my teammates. This was the first kid that was my age that I was actually afraid of. Turns out, she was a terrific running back and linebacker; maybe our best player.

That season did little to lessen my love for football. It fueled the fiery love that I have always had for the sport. I knew I would play for the rest of my life. In Pop's career in the oil field, we moved a lot. From San Antonio to Oklahoma City, back to San Antonio and back to Oklahoma City. We did this a few times until we moved permanently to Alabama in 1984. Our move after my first football season back to Texas put a small obstacle in my football future. Turns out, at the Southwest Optimist Park, you have to weigh over 42 pounds in order to play football in the five and six-year-old division. I had gained some weight but was in the low thirties and they wouldn't make an exception for me to play. I was devastated and my parents were pretty upset about it too. I had to sit out that season but I would find a way to gain the weight required for me to play in second grade.

The following year, I was close enough that I was allowed to play for the Bears. We were black and orange. I was fired up! I was number 35 and played defensive line and tight end, usually reserved for bigger kids. I guess my coaches just needed a place to put the small guy. Our jamboree was coming up and Coach told us to have our pants dyed black and I wanted to get some orange socks. My socks were of regular size, designed to come up to or just over the knee; on a normal sized seven-year-old. Mine came all the way up to my hips and still had to be folded down. My bright orange socks were my mom's way of identifying me while I was playing as if the fact that I was the smallest kid on the field wasn't enough for her.

Jamboree day was the day that I scored my first touchdown in an organized game. This wasn't the typical touchdown. I always had a plan to defeat the kid across from me according to his size. I knew in this game I would have to be quick. Those linemen were huge! If I could anticipate their snap count, I could be in the backfield before the big linemen could get their hands off the ground. When you're seven-years-old, long snap counts aren't a very good idea, so I knew that they would go "on one" every play. I timed it perfectly and before the quarterback could hand the ball off to his running back, I made a pocket with my arms and took the hand off as if it were designed for me and scampered 60 yards for the score! After the game, momma said, "Spunky [my childhood nickname], I knew it was you because of your orange socks. What were you thinking when you took the hand off and was running?"

"I hope I am running to the right end zone", I replied. Of all of my responses to momma's questions over the years, that still remains her favorite answer of all time!

The next year, when I was eight, my size had started to become a little less noticeable. I was still smaller than everyone else, but I was closing the gap. This season, I played for the Tigers and it was the year of nemesis number two, Matt Tullis. Matt was the quarterback and didn't see much need in being close to any of his teammates. He was pretty good; and he knew it. I don't think we won a single game that year but that didn't keep his arrogance from being obvious. After one game that I do remember, we lost 12-6; a parent said to Matt, "You played great Matt". You would think a 'thank you' or a 'we all did' would be the reply. Not with Tullis! His response was an expected, "Don't I always?" In Matt's arrogance, I learned humility. Although I would turn out to be a pretty good player over my life, I never boasted about it and I have Matthew Tullis to thank for that. Arrogance would have been ugly on me.

Chapter Four

Culture Shock; Sooner to Big Al

In November of 1984, momma and Pop informed us that we would be moving to Northport, Alabama; a city just west of Tuscaloosa, the home of the Alabama Crimson Tide. It really wasn't a huge deal since we have moved so many times before. Before this move, I was in the middle of third grade and I had already attended four different schools. Moving and adjusting to a new environment was common for us, so we didn't really have a problem with it. We were leaving behind some good friends, but what's new? My dad was going to work for my Mom's uncle Moody and we were moving to be closer to momma's family who were originally from the area.

I was going to miss my old neighborhoods. I would miss the weeknight Bible studies that my parents held at our house on Telephone Road, where the kids would play outside in our backyard at night. And when I tell you we saw a UFO one night, I mean we saw a UFO. Now, I don't tend to believe in life on other planets or anywhere else—scripture doesn't mention it—but we saw what we saw. It was a bright light spinning and humming. Then, suddenly it went straight up in the air and out of sight. In the places I had lived up until 1984, the landscape was really flat. I didn't know what "the woods" were, never heard the word "forest" and a hill was only something you would come upon every once in a while. Oklahoma was so flat, and known for spring tornadoes, that on some days, you could actually see a tornado that was a hundred miles away. At one point, I remember several Saturdays in a row that we were under tornado warnings.

Now we were moving to another state, and in a region at the foothills of the Appalachian Mountains. I didn't really know what to expect. To begin with, we were going to live in the basement of momma's brother, Allan and his wife, Aunt Von. They had two daughters, Beth, who was a couple of years older than Jackie, and Angela, my cousin who is closest to my age. Angela and I were in the same grade and we remained very close throughout our childhood. Adulthood has spread us all so far apart these days that it is rare that I even get to see anyone anymore. We arrived on a November evening and visited for a little while before we all laid down to rest from the long drive.

The next morning, I walked outside to see the Alabama landscape in the daylight for the first time. Hearing a phrase like, 'It's in the woods' was weird to me. I had never seen woods before. I have seen a tree here and a group of trees there, but never a whole bunch of them. What is even stranger, the first 'woods' that I saw were actually in the biggest neighborhood in the state of Alabama at that time. Woods, in a neighborhood? I was in awe. My aunt took us on a tour of the city of Northport, Tuscaloosa and the University of Alabama that night. As we crossed a bridge over the Black Warrior River, she pointed to the west and said' "That is Cypress Inn Restaurant, it is on the river". Well, I thought it was actually ON the river—like floating. I thought that was so cool; until I realized it was just on the banks of the river. It was like we had moved to a foreign country and the language was different. What I had always called 'kickball' was called 'kick pen' in Alabama. I couldn't figure out why, and as a Physical Education teacher in Alabama today, I STILL don't know why and I still refuse to call it that.

During the tour of campus, I got to see a lot of cool things. Memorial Coliseum, now known as Coleman Coliseum, Denny Chimes and Bryant Denny Stadium, which was a lot smaller than it is today. I really wasn't impressed; I was a Sooner fan! It was around Thanksgiving and football season was almost over. I can't remember if we were in Alabama in time for the 'Iron Bowl', the annual clash between the Alabama Crimson Tide and the Auburn Tigers. I never really heard much about the rivalry until we moved. My first experience with the Iron Bowl came in 1985. We went to the "Quad" on the campus and watched the game on a huge screen with hundreds of people. The crowds out at the Quad were nothing like they are today. It was different to say the least.

I had almost finished my first semester of the 4th grade at Crestmont Elementary School, my second school already in Alabama. I finished third grade at Vestavia Elementary. Most of the kids I was around were rabid Alabama fans and a few held allegiances to the other state school, Auburn. I felt like the few Auburn fans really took a lot of heat from the Alabama faithful and it bothered me. I chose to align myself with the Auburn kids for the 1985 Iron Bowl just because they were outnumbered and I liked beating the odds. Paul Bear Bryant hadn't been gone from Alabama too long and the expectations for Coach Ray Perkins were kind of unattainable. But Alabama was good; not Sooner good, but good.

As we watched the Iron Bowl, on the campus of the Crimson Tide, I wore a faded orange Auburn sweatshirt and annoyed the Alabama fans as much as I could. Auburn led late, but Alabama fought back and got in field goal range for kicker, Van Tiffin. Then, as I was pushing the buttons of Tide fans, "The Kick" happened. From fifty-two yards away, Van Tiffin crushed the hearts of War Eagle Nation. I had no idea what 'bandwagon' meant and I didn't know what it meant to 'jump ship', but that's what I did! This was the night that I became a full-fledged Alabama Crimson Tide fan. Bandwagon fandom irritates me today, but I was 9, I didn't know any better and since that day I have been able to celebrate several national championships as a fan and had I stayed faithful to Auburn; well, only one! We did have a stretch of painful years though.

The thought started to occur to me during this time that neither Alabama's nor Auburn's mascot or war cry fit their name. What does an elephant have to do with a big red wave or red rising waters? And what does 'War Eagle' have to do with a Tiger? It was all confusing to me. I've since learned the answers to both, but I will leave you to research that for yourself. I felt like I was betraying my Sooner friends, but whom in Oklahoma knew? There was no social media to show your entire identity on. It was my secret; Brian 'Boz' Bosworth would never find out. I was safe; from Sooner to Big Al.

Chapter Five

Experience Beats Age

As we moved to Alabama, all I could think of was, "What kind of football do they have for my age?" When we arrived in November of 1984, little league football season was over so we had to do some calling around to find our where to go and when. Through investigation, we learned that in the West Alabama Youth Football League, a player had to be ten-years-old to play. I wasn't even nine yet, but would be by the time registration rolled around. I held on to hope that they would make an exception for me. The hope I held on to was limited, though. I was still really little. I wasn't bigger than many kids my age and my size was noticeable. Now, we had to wait until registration in July of 1985 to find out if they would allow me to play. One look at me, the answer was sure to be 'No'.

As I mentioned, we were living in my Aunt and Uncle's basement in the largest neighborhood I had ever seen. The first entrance to Northwood Lake was just past the major intersection of U.S. Highway 82 and Alabama Highway 69, maybe one hundred fifty yards away. The last entrance was nearly four miles up 69. Then from the Highway 69 entrances, Northwood

Lake Subdivision stretched all the way to U.S. Highway 43 about a mile and a half west. Just to give you a visual of the size of this place, I have seen areas with its own zip codes that were smaller.

Uncle Alan and Aunt Von's house was on a cul-de-sac street and in the middle of the circled street was a portable basketball goal with a dirt court. I was wondering if we were in Indiana or Kentucky. I never saw any kids in that circle playing football. I mean, I was now living right in the middle of football country, in the football capital of the world, and there were no kids on my new street playing football. Now that I think about it, I rarely saw anyone playing basketball out there either. Our street only had about six houses on it and I don't remember any kids living in any of them; none that I played outside with anyway.

It was an adjustment for me to say the least. In Oklahoma City and San Antonio, I lived in neighborhoods that had straight streets, dozens of kids and constantly something to do outside. Although Northwood Lake was huge, getting from one area to the next wasn't easy because the main roads through the subdivision were busy; like highways. It was hard to walk from one street to the next and it couldn't even be done without walking onto one of the busy thoroughfares. I didn't like it very much and spent most of my time in the house—with two sisters and two female cousins—bored to death.

My two favorite items that I owned were a stuffed clown that I bought for a quarter at a garage sale and a big stuffed gorilla. "Lickety-Slappity" and "Monk" were soon to become my best friends and playmates. Living in San Antonio and Oklahoma City, kids had a fondness of wrestling. In both cities, wrestling was a big part of life. In these cities, you didn't have to wait for a wrestling federation to come to town, they were there every week. I remember times when my parents would put us all in the car, not telling us where we were going or lying about it—we are going to buy light bulbs, or we were going to Luby's Cafeteria to eat supper—and just start driving. We would pass one Luby's, the Otasco Store where we bought light bulbs and into downtown OKC by the oil derricks on the Capitol lawn. Pulling into Hemisphere arena, we knew it was time for some Southwest Championship Wresting or World Class Championship Wrestling. Didn't matter to us which federation it was, we loved it!

One time, Pop tried to keep the secret all the way into the door of the arena by saying we were going to the "Ice Capades"—whatever that was, but as we pulled in to the parking area, I could tell the difference in Oklahoma wrestling fans and people who would purposely attend an ice skating event. It was obvious—we were there to see some wrestling. The closest we ever got to ringside was on a night that I witnessed the bloodiest match I have ever seen—until I was introduced to Bruiser Brody and Abdullah the Butcher and their "Fork Matches". It was gruesome. One time, I put a picture from one of my wrestling magazines on the refrigerator to scare Shara. It was a full page, color picture of Abdullah the Butcher, post match, bloody, bald and scary. It was hilarious watching Shara walk into the kitchen and quickly run out, crying!

The bloody match included The Freebirds, who was the most popular group of the time, and Bobby Jaggers and the Sheepherders; later to become the Bushwhackers of the WWF, in a six-man tag team match. Michael PS Hayes, Terry Bam Bam Gordy and Buddy Phillips made up the Freebirds and they were the bad guys, but I loved them. Jaggers and the Herders were the good guys but I only liked Jaggers. Bobby Jaggers had long blonde hair and very weak skin on his forehead. As we sat really close to ringside, the match went on and was exciting until the Sheepherders turned on Jaggers during the match and beat him with a flag pole that they used to display their New Zealand flag. Jaggers was busted open as the Freebirds watched in enjoyment. Bobby's blonde hair was covered in blood and his limp body began twitching as he bled. It was scary, especially since my sisters and I were faithful believers in the realness of the sport.

That is my most vivid memory of live wrestling spectating. Wrestling was a huge part of my life and the culture of the neighborhoods that I lived in. Regional to National promotions readily available to attend every Saturday night and we lived really close to several pro wrestlers when we lived in San Antonio. Scott Casey, my favorite wrestler at the time, lived on a ranch really close to us. Pop would drive me by there periodically just so I could see it and hope to see Scott on a tractor or one of his horses. My Aunt Paula, momma's only sister, got involved in wrestling through our love for the sport. She actually ended up getting really involved as she became a "valet"—or a female manager—for a couple of the wrestlers that I loved to follow. She feuded with female wrestlers that I had known for a while. It was awesome to have a family member in the sport that I loved to watch.

Anyway, back on the cul-de-sac in Northwood Lake. Through my boredom of not having any backyard football games to play in, and the lack of boys on my street, momma would bring me some wrestling magazines to help me pass the time in a house full of girls. Most of my evenings included wrestling matches between me and Lickety-Slappity and Monk. I would learn new moves from the magazines and practice them on my lifeless friends. I would commentate the matches like I was Gordon Solie or Jim Ross—famous wrestling broadcasters of the 1980's. It's all I had to do. I was so ready for football season so I would know if I would be able to play. I played my first season of baseball in Alabama at Kentuck Park in the spring of 1985. I played for the Rams and we were undefeated and won the championship. These guys in Alabama could play some baseball! I was out of my league; wishing football would hurry and get here!

Finally, in the summer of 1985, at nine-years-old, the West Alabama Youth Football League (WAYFL) initially said that couldn't play until I was ten. Momma and Pop pleaded with the board to make an exception because I had three years of playing experience and the ten-year-olds had none. After the board met, it was determined that if the coach of the Northport Wildcats was okay with me playing, then I could play. I couldn't have spent a second football season sitting and watching over what I felt like was a small technicality. First, I was too small, and now too young? I was going to show them a thing or two about debilitating technicalities! I was registered; ready to play!

Coach Glen Milligan was my coach. Still to this day, I have a great relationship with his family and his son, Joey, who played for the Senior Team, is the man that I owe for getting me into high school coaching. Joey is one of my closest friends and someone who I consider a huge factor in my faith and my accountability. Being able to be around Christian coaches in a field that lacks this dynamic is amazing! Bible studies in the Coaches Office were the norm when we coached together. Joey is an example to me and the other coaches of a Faith First approach to mentoring and coaching young men. He stresses self-motivation to players and us coaches. His approach to coaching is what I model my own approach from and I owe this man a lot.

I was the youngest player in the entire WAYFL, and one of the smallest. But my aggressive attitude caught the attention of the coaches and I was a practice All-Star that year. Coach Jimmy Burns was the assistant coach and the man who gave me my first opportunity to coach when I was just nineteen-years-old. He made me the Head Coach of the nine and ten-year-old team in 1995. Apparently after I showed the league that a nine-year-old could play with older kids back in 1985, they decided to restructure the age requirements and even added a flag football league for younger kids to develop them and give them some experience. I didn't get a ton of playing time that year, but I got enough. I made my presence known every day at practice getting the starters ready to play; some hated me for it, some loved me, but I knew what my job was and I did it. Although the deck was stacked against me, I proved that experience was better than age and it was that season that I, and my family, all realized that God blessed me with the ability to play football; and He made me small for a reason.

Chapter Six

Sunscreen Faith

There are so many Christians that have the luxury of explaining that they grew up in church and have always followed Christ. That is a great testimony. For someone to be raised that way, go to secular schools, deal with peer pressures, become an adult and still have a hold on the promises of Jesus through all of it is something amazing. That testimony is quite powerful in the Great Commission. My testimony is much different. My parents were always believers. My dad was raised in a large Lutheran Church in Texas and mom was raised Baptist. I was raised a "Sporadic". I know, no one has ever heard of such a denomination. What I mean is my family was sporadic in our church attendance. We went in chunks. I think my parents struggled a bit about where God wanted them serving.

My earliest memories of church-going were stints in Pentecostal churches and country Baptist churches. My dad had a lot of problems and it is sometimes hard to find a church that is accepting of a man; and his

29

problems. That may have had something to do with my never having a constant church attendance pattern. Pop was on the road a lot as well with almost every job he had, so it was a tough deal on momma. What my family lacked in church attendance, they didn't lack in their love for Jesus. They were always teaching us things that they knew from scripture. Momma had this uninterrupted love for all of us and she could only get that type of heart from one thing; a heart full of Jesus.

When we moved to Alabama, I remember our church attendance being a little more settled, especially after momma graduated from nursing school. We attended Northport Church of God and I loved it. I heard a man from our church explain to someone in the grocery store while inviting him to church, "We could be considered to be 'highly-caffeinated' Christians". That description is humorous, but accurate! It was great, never a dull moment. Pastor James Hockensmith was a little up in his years, but his energy and caffeinating delivery of his sermons made me not want to attend any youth services. I would rather be in 'Big Church' listening to him. It was here that I felt the first sparking of the Holy Spirit in my heart; an unexplained lump in my throat and weakening in my arms and legs.

I "gave my heart to Jesus". Or did I really? I was definitely what I call a sunscreen Christian with sunscreen faith. The kids in my youth ministry always laugh at my strange ways of explaining things. What is a Sunscreen Christian? Well, I am a fair-skinned man. My skin burns fairly easily when exposed to the dangers of the sun. I also despise lotions, sprays, cologne, perfume, candles and honestly anything with a chemically enhanced smell to it. It took a lot for me to actually apply sunscreen to my skin. I resisted as much as I could; just up until the time it was critically needed. My limping walk with Christ was the same way. I didn't like what being a Christian meant to my habits. I never took much time praying; none really. Now and then, I would be in such need of something from Him that I would FINALLY go to Him and ask; but it took a lot for me to do so, much like the application of sunscreen. I would use God; or seek him in an attempt to thwart of whatever danger I was facing at the moment.

That is basically the description of my faith as a teenager. I avoided a lot of activities that would require me being around kids of faith because of the guilt that I felt in the way I was actually living. My faith was more centered on football and popularity. I had several Christian friends but I would gravitate more to the ones that condoned the things I was doing, and would participate with me. Faith in Christ wasn't in my everyday thoughts as a child and a teenager. I was a distraction in school and disrespect towards teachers became what I was known for in elementary school and early in junior high. My behavior was a direct reflection of my avoidance of Jesus in my life.

As I grew older, the moment that I accepted Jesus was completely gone from my conscience. It went from a rare thought to complete absence. I have always believed in the Gospel and Jesus, but it was an afterthought to me. Momma was still trying to get me to increase my attention to God's call on my life, but it usually—in her words—went in one ear and out the other. I had the assumption that I didn't have any time for Jesus. I was so focused on football and neighborhood fights that I had no time for anything else. From the time that I was ten until I finished playing football, the sport was my top priority and not much else mattered. I had a lot of faith, but it was in myself and my abilities to play football, though I was still small. I would later find out that the things I put all of my faith in were usually removed from my life either by my own idiotic mistakes or God's intervention; and today, I couldn't be more thankful for anything else.

Royce C. Brehm

Chapter Seven

From the Basement to the Top of the Hill

In the summer of 1985, my parents were able to move us out of the basement in Northwood Lake. My great grandfather, Victor Mitchell, who played football at Auburn University in the late 1800's lived in a different section of Northport known as Gold Star Acres. He lived at the top of a hill in a red house and on his property was a green building that we just knew as the "Garage Apartment". No one lived there, it was just used for junk and storage for things Granddaddy didn't want to throw away. Nana was living with him at the time because he was in his upper nineties, yet he was still very active. Granddaddy loved working outdoors. It was not uncommon to see him climbing a pecan tree because he had already picked up the pecans that were on the ground. He was just that tough. He cut his own grass and did just about everything on his own until he fell from one of those trees and spent a small time in a nursing home just prior to passing away.

Granddaddy was a tall man. His ears resembled small satellites but it wasn't something that I chose to mention to him. He was a mountain of a man. He had a bed in his living room that he called his day bed and I would sit there while the Price is Right was on the television, muted of course, and he would tell me stories of his childhood. My favorite stories were those about him playing football at Auburn. The fact that my great grandfather

32

played for the Tigers never impacted my decision to be an Alabama fan after Auburn allowed Van Tiffin to kick that field goal in November of '85. But I enjoyed his stories nonetheless.

Across the street from Granddaddy's house was a small gray house with two front doors. That was strange to me and it didn't help when momma explained to me that the house used to be a 'duplex'. That didn't mean a lot to me. This was where we would be moving. The house was kind of run down and the heaters were in the middle of the floor in the living room and kitchen. This was a home set up that I had never seen before. To get from the kitchen to the back part of the house, my parent's bedroom and my sisters' bedroom, you had to walk through what was going to be my bedroom. I didn't really like the place.

But things started to look brighter as I looked out the back window to see that we were going to have a backyard, slightly sloped, and big enough for some great tackle football games. The only question I had was, 'How many kids live around here and do they play football?' I only knew of adults that lived on that street. Momma's uncle Earl and Aunt Kaye lived right next door and all of their kids were grown up. I was hoping that there were some football players down the road in the other direction. I remember walking outside and to the left where I saw what looked like apartments, but some of the buildings were single family dwellings and some were what Momma called duplexes and some were two-levels with two front doors. I was told that that neighborhood was "The Projects". Now, I only knew of projects in school; science and social studies. I never knew of an apartment community known as The Projects. I wasn't quite sure what that was.

The first kid I met was Jason, an African-American kid that lived in the first unit which was right next door to us. In the places I had lived before, including Northwood Lake, I didn't have many interactions with kids from another race. In San Antonio we had many Mexican kids, but rarely did I see any black kids. I wasn't real sure how to act towards them. Jason took me to his apartment to introduce me to his mother, Doretha. Ms. Doretha had a candy rack in the living room where she sold candy to neighborhood kids. I couldn't believe what I was seeing. I didn't know what a Now-And-Later was, but I was willing to try! And those crunchy peanut butter sticks were incredible. Jason told his mom bye and we walked down the street as he explained that we were going to see an elderly woman that sells frozen Kool aid from her apartment. These were known to the kids as "Freezer Cups" and for some odd reason, they were much better than if I had frozen my own Kool Aid.

Jason introduced me to several kids in Knoll Circle, the name of the housing development. Almost every one of them quickly asked, "Are you related to Mr. Mitchell?"—Granddaddy was known to everyone in Knoll Circle as Mr. Mitchell. Everyone was scared of him. Granddaddy grew up in an era that saw a lot of racism and as mean as he seemed, he was a little further along in his acceptance of other races than many of the people that were from his time. He lived in harmony with his surroundings, except if someone—anyone—walked across his yard.

Everyone in Knoll Circle walked to school. Elementary kids attended Crestmont Elementary which was about half-a-mile away and cutting across granddaddy's yard made the trip a lot shorter and he didn't approve. Some days he would sit on his front porch in his rocking chair with his .22 rifle in his lap and he wasn't scared to fire a shot in the air to get the traffic to cease. It got to the point that the junior high and high school kids took a different route to Northport Junior High and Tuscaloosa County High—which were both over a mile away—just to avoid the temptation of walking through granddaddy's yard. As I learned of the neighborhood's relationship with "Mr. Mitchell", I wondered if this would make my life here tough; or would it protect me since he was so feared and respected?

The set up kind of went both ways. I being small and the only white kid in the neighborhood had more to do with my reputation than who my great-grandfather was. I began to build some really good relationships with kids in Knoll Circle. Jason remained the one I was closest to. I got in at least one good fight with every kid there, except Jason. We did have this one "falling out" that took some time to heal. I found a turtle in the creek at the bottom of the hill and made it a great home from a box. I am sure I named the guy, but I don't remember what it was and I sure didn't put a collar on him. For the sake of the story, we will call the turtle "Shelly". One day Shelly was missing. I put his box in the backyard because my parents wouldn't let me keep him inside because he didn't smell great and his claws rubbing against that cardboard box was nothing short of annoying.

I looked all over the place for Shelly but couldn't find him. I was told later that day as I employed the help of friends in the search for Shelly that Jason got a turtle too. I went and looked and his new pet looked identical to Shelly! Of course if you've seen one Alabama box turtle, you've seen them all and there was just no way to know if the two were the same. But I was accusing and Jason was defending. I said it was Shelly, he said it wasn't. It caused quite a stink between the two of us and even his family and mine. I still don't have any proof that his turtle was Shelly, but he never supplied any proof that it wasn't. But we remained friends and through social media channels, we still are.

I could write a one-thousand-page book about my time at the top of the hill, but for time's sake I will hit the high points and the most memorable times. Of course, my favorite thing to do was to play backyard football. Lonzell was an older kid and insanely athletic. He was left-handed and could throw a football from one end of my yard over two or three other yards. He was lightning fast too and his size was pretty intimidating. But I backed down from no one, including Lonzell. Ronnie or Junior as he was known to us — was the big hitter and his aiming point was always the knees. I suffered a few minor injuries from the two of them and I am pretty fortunate that I never broke any bones in those games.

I was definitely the smallest kid and obviously the only white kid so you would have a pretty good idea of where in the order I was picked when it came time to choose teams? Traditionally, it would be safe to assume that I was last unless a girl showed up to play. But that wasn't the case at all. If

Royce C. Brehm

Lonzell and Junior were the Captains, I was picked first by one of them. If they weren't captains, I usually got picked right after they did. They all saw me as an asset to their team and I usually produced. I was never scared.

Some days after we were finished playing, we would run next door and buy some candy and go back to my yard, climb a tree and make up rap lyrics, usually with a heavy comedic tone. My sisters loved to come outside and hear us rap our lyrics and "jank" each other. Jank was the term used at the time for "making fun of a friend or pointing out their flaws" and my friends were really good at it. One rap song that I still remember was "Jankin' Time" where we would all start with 'A janky janky, a janky time…uh what ya say…' followed by someone's best attempt at a jank. We went in order so there was some flow to it. "All You Can Eat" was one of my sisters' favorites and every now and then, that song still comes up in our conversations.

Leviticus was a year or two older than me. He was a really tall kid and was pretty good at basketball. LV, as we called him was from Buffalo, New York and the rough living of Knoll Circle was easy for him. He had seen worse in New York. LV was one of the best "jank rappers" in the neighborhood. His wise cracks were sometimes aimed at me being the small white boy, but I laughed just as hard as everyone else. Of all of my friends from Knoll Circle, I am still closest to him these days. We differ on a lot of political views today, but we still find humor in calling each other out on them. LV works in security these days in large cities—Pittsburgh as of today—but when he was in Nashville, I would go up for Predators hockey games especially when they played against his beloved Buffalo Sabres. We jokingly argued about that too; until his last place Sabres defeated my first place Predators.

Nikia and Davey were brothers. They were just a year apart in age. The time I spent with them usually consisted of making clubhouses out of old wood and whatever else we could find. We would strategically use the ditch at the bottom of the hill as the base of our clubhouse unless it was wet with rain. Those clubhouses came and went because of the rain and older kids having a blast by tearing it down just to be mean. I've lost contact with Nikia and Davey over the years, but I really love the memories that I had with them.

Tchaka and Titus were Junior's younger brothers. I spent a lot of time with Tchaka, probably more than anyone else. He was usually the kid that I was most likely to get in a fight with and the most likely to start a fight with someone else that I would end up involved in. I think my time hanging out with "Shocka" is where I received a lot of my toughness from. If I was with him close to the time I was supposed to be home, I could almost guarantee that I would have to fight to get home. Over time, we would venture outside of our neighborhood into other streets and get into fights there. None of this was terrible in nature, just a few altercations with people that weren't enemies. Usually the whole situation was over with and forgotten before we walked away.

Fighting became fun for me. I started to get the same adrenaline rush from fighting as I did from playing football. I loved it and at times I craved it. I began to develop quite a reputation in the area as a violent kid and I fed off of that. I would fight anyone, anywhere and whenever I could—and I did, quite often. I never numbered the fights, never kept a record of winning or losing, and I never held a grudge with the opponent. It was almost hobby-like. The enjoyment I got from fighting carried with me through most of my life and I lived a very violent life at times. I rarely got into a fight when I was angry. In a way, that is sad to say because it wasn't emotional for me, it was habitual. I couldn't let much time go by before I started another one. It started out as something I felt like I had to do in order to establish the fact that although I was a small white kid living in an African-American community, I was not intimidated and I needed to make sure that I could get home every afternoon. At times, I literally had to fight just to get home on time.

I have developed friendships throughout my life in different settings, but none like the ones I had in Knoll Circle in the mid-to-late 1980's. My time there had plenty to do with my toughness and my ability to play football and protect myself. I learned, out of necessity, that it is important to get along with everyone, even people of different races. My time there allowed me to live a life that has been free of racism and division. Financially for my family, it wasn't the best of times as my mom went to school and Pop worked all over the south, but the lessons I learned and the memories I made were very valuable. It is still humorous to me when I see or talk to one of my old friends from Knoll Circle and we end our conversation or electronic communication with "KCP 4 LIFE" and I, the little white boy can still say that I am indeed "Knoll Circle Posse for Life".

Chapter Eight

"Quitty's Back"

Throughout my time at the top of the hill, I still played organized football for WAYFL and I started to grow; a little bit. I played baseball too and I was decent at it. I played centerfield most seasons and I was able to make some really good catches and I had a pretty strong throwing arm. I was not very good at the plate though. I couldn't hit really well and it was usually feast or famine in my at-bats. If I didn't hit the ball to the fence, I struck out—badly. I definitely struck out more times than anything else. One thing that I was never able to do was pitch. I tried. I was really good at my imaginary pitching starts in the Little League World Series with the block wall of our basement as my catcher. I mean, how could I mess that up? I called the balls and strikes and I would determine when an opponent got on base!

At Kentuck Park in Northport, if you wanted to make All-Stars, you had better be a pitcher. A good centerfielder with a less than stellar batting average wasn't good enough to play the extended season and travel all summer playing in different cities in Alabama. It started to really bother me that this was the case and I stopped loving baseball and after finishing the last year I was eligible to play at the park, I quit playing except for the two years I played for the high school summer league just for the fun of it. Football was my passion!

I made All Stars I football for the Northport Wildcats every year I played—except that first year when I was supposed to be too young. All Stars in football consisted of one game, between the southern teams in the league against the northern teams. It was a fun time. I loved going and practicing with kids that I played against during the season, especially since we always won the league championship. One year, somehow Northport got grouped in the southern teams for the All Star game and practice was to be held in Moundville, a town about 15 miles south of Tuscaloosa and twenty miles away from home. Six to Eight of my teammates were on the All Star team and for all of us to get to practice together, we all piled in the back of Coach Burns' truck and rode the twenty-something miles in the freezing weather of November.

I was able to do some really neat things in my little league football time. My mom's favorite memory was against the Tuscaloosa Tigers when I was 12. I kicked off to start the second half and instead of doing the traditional thing for the kicker and sitting back as a safety just in case the kick was returned passed all of our defenders, I flew down field and almost knocked the ball carrier's helmet off. He fumbled as a result and I recovered it. I was also the fullback and on the very next play, I took the handoff and ran thirty-something yards for the touchdown. The next play, I kicked the 'point after touchdown' or the extra point as its known to most people. Then I repeated the kickoff scenario, except this time the return man didn't fumble. I still love hearing momma tell that story, and she still likes telling it.

I played in the WAYFL for as many years as I was allowed, six total. When I turned 14, I had to play for Northport Junior High. It was my ninth grade year and it was my first to play there so I didn't really expect to play very much. And I didn't. I played a total of two games. I ended up being the back up fullback and the plans were for me to get a few carries every game and come in as a blocker for Steve, the best football player I ever knew. The first game went well. I got a few carries and made some key blocks that allowed Steve to score several touchdowns. Steve was a man among boys. In 9th grade he was over six-feet tall and weighed about 210 pounds. He was fast as a deer and when you get that much weight running as fast as he did, it was nearly impossible to tackle him. I think he was actually tackled only four times that entire game. It was incredible.

The next game was against our cross town rival Riverside. Riverside had a long time coach, Coach Griffin and we had long time legend, Coach Aaron. These two men coached at these two schools for decades. I admire both men a great deal. I hated that I missed that game. I hurt my knee the day before the game and wasn't cleared to play. I was devastated. For football players in Northport, you look forward to playing in that game and then you dream of playing for Tuscaloosa County High against Central Tuscaloosa. These games were what dreams were made of for us, and I was missing it. I don't even remember if we won or lost.

Game three rolled around the following Thursday as we traveled across the Black Warrior River to play Hillcrest. Today, Hillcrest is a rival of the Northport schools but back then, they were just another opponent. I was excited to be back on the field for that game. Just as Steve rarely got tackled, in that game, I didn't get tackled at all. Granted, I only had two carries but those two carries netted me one hundred thirty yards and two touchdowns. After the game I was the last player to get on the bus and the whole team gave me the traditional dog-pile which usually occurred outside, on the field, on the soft grass not on the hard floor of a school bus. It didn't matter to me. I just saw the future of the season and Steve and I scoring at will and beating everybody!

The next Monday at practice as we were preparing to play Bibb County, I was tackled. As I landed on the dirt of the softball field that we practiced on, I caught myself right on my right elbow and the sound of breaking bone gave the whole team a nauseous stomach. My humorous bone fractured from the elbow all the way up to where it connects at the shoulder. Immediately the swelling caused any definition in my arm to disappear. I was finished. I was taken into our fieldhouse where they began to ice my elbow and try to calm me down. The pain was intense but it wasn't the biggest of pains for me at that time. My season was over. That fact is what brought on the tears I was crying.

The Tuscaloosa County High football team practiced on the field behind our field house and our back doors were open for their players during their water breaks. The high school players were like celebrities to us and I was really worried about them seeing me cry as they began to walk in to cool off. Much to my amazement, guys I admired greatly began to encourage me and Dustin, a big lineman that went to play for the Crimson Tide told me it would be ok, I would heal and be playing with him next year. That was all the motivation I needed to dry up he tears and prepare to rehabilitate and get on the field with guys that I considered to be heroes.

This was the year after I met the guy who would end up being my best friend. We were nearly inseparable from eighth grade all the way through high school and today, although we are busy and have families, we are still best friends. At the beginning of the eighth grade while we were in PE class, I noticed a new kid shooting basketball. He was a left-handed shooter and he was making shots from all over the floor. I couldn't believe how good this guy was at something that I was terrible at doing. I didn't speak to him for a few days but continued to be in awe of his ability to play basketball.

For about a week, he would play basketball and sit at lunch with some guys that were not in the group of friends that I was in, but I really wanted to introduce myself to him just to see where he was from and to see if he played football because I have never been a big fan of basketball. I figured any guy that is as athletic as he was would have to be a football player. So the day came when I finally went up to him and informed him that he had been hanging out with unpopular kids—even though they weren't really unpopular, but pretty cool, just weren't in my group. His response was, "They live in my neighborhood and my parents are making me hang out with them." Sounded like a lame excuse to me and I later found out, it was.

He started hanging out with my group of friends and from then on, we were like brothers. Spring Training in football was quickly approaching and it was time to prepare for what would be my injury shortened season. I wasn't used to spring training and didn't really know what to expect. I convinced my new best friend to come out and give football a try. The first day didn't go well for him as the coaching staff put him with the offensive line while he felt he should have been a tight end. He quit that day and my barrage of insults began as quickly as he quit. I gave him the nickname "Quitty". I spent the next day trying my best to make him feel bad and I guess it worked.

The following afternoon at practice as I was getting in our stretching lines, I felt a tapping on my helmet. When I turned around, there he was in full football gear ready to practice. All he said was, "Quitty's back!" Lucky for us at Northport Junior High and later at Tuscaloosa County High, he reconsidered because he went on to be a great offensive lineman and made the All-State team our senior year. Quitty's name is Reggie Plowman and for many years, we were actually known as one entity. When people wondered where one of us was, the question was 'Where are Royce and Reggie?' In April 2017, I was honored to officiate his wedding, a private service in the youth room at my church. Everyone needs a best friend in their life growing up. Rarely do those kinds of friendships last throughout one's life. As I said, we both live really busy lives and we live a fair distance apart, but to this day, we are still "Royce and Reggie".

Chapter Nine

From Heroes to Teammates

My ninth grade year was coming to an end and we had been walking across the street to Tuscaloosa County High in the afternoons for training sessions with their players and coaches. Spring training was coming and it was time to play football with all of those older guys that I looked at like celebrities. Coach Norrell had been the head coach for a few years and he was known as hardcore conditioning coach. He wanted to always put conditioned athletes on the field. It was a very tough adjustment from just a few sprints at the end of every practice to running stadium steps in the heat and THEN running sprints. I was once again one of the smallest players on the team and I had to do whatever I could to prove that I belonged. I ran every step as hard as I could, ran every sprint as fast as I could and tried my best to catch the attention of the coaching staff as well as the older players.

One afternoon as we walked across the track into the parking lot on our way to the stadium for another training session, a couple of the upcoming seniors ran out to us and excitedly informed us that Coach Norrell was leaving and the new coach, Coach Moore didn't believe in the same kind of conditioning; he liked to "practice his players into shape"; meaning he ran tough practices that served to get us into playing shape. I knew they were excited about that, but the first thought that crossed my mind was 'How are tough practices better than running in the offseason without pads and a helmet on?' It didn't matter to me because I knew it was business as usual—catch the coaches' attention.

The time came for incoming players to sign up for the position that we wanted to try out for during spring training. I had been a fullback for years and hadn't played very much defense, sparingly at best. I knew fullback wasn't the spot for me because the one they had returning was known as Chris the "Northport Nightmare". He was big; about one hundred pounds more than me and his size, playing style and ability was well suited for Coach Moore's double wing offense. In this style of offense, the fullback is usually behind the quarterback all by himself and most of his carries would come from the inside, in a scrum of humans and it would be almost impossible for me to be effective there due to my lack of stature.

The wide receiver position in this offense was actually better suited for me because I loved to block and did so pretty well. I rarely ever had to catch a pass, but in this case, I wouldn't have to worry about it much because my job would be to block! That's what I signed up for but not where I ended up. After a couple of spring practices, I was catching some attention from coaches and older players. In scrimmages and drills against the defense, I was being really aggressive and it was aggravating some of the juniors and seniors. I would start a small altercation now and then just to get all the attention on me. With over one hundred players, that seemed to be the best course of action to achieve what I was looking for.

My aggressive practice style caught the attention of the defensive coaches and I was approached by Coach McNabb, a veteran coach of the outside linebackers. He told me that they wanted me to practice on the defensive side of the ball for the rest of the spring. We had almost twenty wide receivers and the outside linebacker position only had six. I saw this as a perfect opportunity to move up the depth chart, regardless of what side of the ball it was on. I had played defense before, but rather sparingly but it excited me to be able to be in a position to be aggressive and it actually be normal and accepted.

The annual spring game was coming up the following week. The Blue White Game is the conclusion of Spring Practices and was a split squad scrimmage game with bragging rights on the line. The two teams were split up and if you were in one of the top two spots on the depth chart, you get a chance to start the game for your team. I spent the next week trying to catch up on what I missed at my new position and trying to climb that depth chart. I wanted to start that game! I guess I did enough because when the depth charts were updated and the teams were announced, I was second team outside linebacker and was a starter for the white team. I was fired up! I had worked so hard to overcome my small size with determination and aggression. I had known that I had angered a few of the older players in the past and this game would surely be their opportunity to get me back.

At the time, I weighed maybe one hundred-thirty-five pounds—with my pads on. Tuscaloosa County High was the seventh largest school in the entire state and had some really large humans on our roster. The team I was on consisted of mostly second team defensive players with the first team offense. Although I wouldn't be across the ball from Dustin, Clay and the other first team monsters on offense, the second team guys were huge as well. But I didn't care. I was not going to back down from them either. I don't remember much about that game or if we won or not, but I do remember that this was the day that I fell deeper in love with football than I ever have and my work ethic was ramped up tenfold.

Coach McNabb took a liking to me and invested a lot of time in making me a better player. Of all of the players on our one-hundred-man roster, he saw something in me, small or otherwise, he saw something. He would lecture me about dipping tobacco, letting girls interfere with my training and he talked a lot about Jesus. Most of his lectures did like my mom described as 'in one ear and out the other'. That was basically the theme of people advising me on life things; I simply didn't listen. I was addicted to tobacco, chased girls and left Jesus as far in the back of my mind as I could so I wouldn't feel convicted about not following Him. But for a year, Coach McNabb stayed in my face about living right and working hard.

Unfortunately for me, Coach McNabb left us after my sophomore season to join the staff at Central-Tuscaloosa; our hated rivals. I was devastated. The one man that invested time and faith in me was gone, and at Central! His departure could have caused me to shut down my work ethic, but it actually did the opposite. Although he was across the river, at THAT school, I wanted to make him proud of me and I felt like I owed him a lot for having confidence in me, so I worked even harder. I wanted to beat him in the annual cross river game that we played at the University of Alabama's Bryant-Denney Stadium; which we hadn't been able to do in several years. Coach McNabb always checked up on me throughout my playing days. When social media became prevalent and I had begun coaching, he checked up on me almost weekly until he passed away recently. Any time I would receive a message from him telling me he was proud of me and my work for the Kingdom of God, I would swell up with pride, more so because he noticed the work I did in Jesus' name than for my success in coaching.

Throughout my time of being away from my relationship with Jesus, people would pop in and out of my life in order to encourage me to get back on the right path. God regularly used these people to correct me and I just wasn't listening to it. Many gave up on me, Coach McNabb never did. In 2013, my defense at Hale County High was in the top three in every statistical category and he messaged me to tell me congratulations and that he knew football would be the way I would make a living. But he spent more time congratulating me on the growth of my youth ministry at Moundville Baptist. Coach McNabb was the reason I moved to defense and he is a huge reason that I live for Christ in ALL that I do today. I owe him much and one day, I will tell him!

Chapter Ten

Look at All That WHITE!!

During my ninth grade year at Northport Junior High, I was suspended for a total of thirty-one days. Most of my suspensions were because I still enjoyed fighting, even during the time my arm was broken. Some other times I had the free day at home were from my disrespect to teachers. I wasn't a very good kid, to say the least. The punishment I received at home never lasted very long as I was right back in Principal Johnson's office getting yet another pink slip of paper informing my parents that I needed chores to do during the next three to five school days. Towards the end of the year, I was tired of the suspensions and decided to take my fights off campus to the nearest church parking lot.

One day, I brought home another pink slip that I had received for fighting at the church—off campus. Pop wasn't happy with me; but he wasn't happy with the suspension either. Pop went to the school and met with Mr. Johnson and I was reinstated, but Pop let me know in his loving, scary way that I had better stop all the nonsense even if I was off campus. He started telling me that I would eventually lose football if I kept making bad decisions and that started to sink in. After years of letting everything 'go in one ear and out the other', the thought of not being able to play football was what it took for me to start thinking about staying out of trouble. I was placing football at the center of everything I did; it was my god.

After my sophomore season and the departure of Coach McNabb, I was wondering how my junior season would look; what position would I play, where I would be on the depth chart and who would be the new defensive coordinator. The uncertainty was scary but I was behaving. I didn't get into any trouble at school my entire sophomore year. The only fights I had were scuffles on the weekend that didn't really have any impact on anything. Football was keeping out of trouble, for the most part anyway. I still had some growing up to do. I had grown a little tired of disappointing my parents and being somewhat of an embarrassment to them. I was getting closer and closer to loving something so much that I didn't want to lose it. My god was football.

One afternoon before spring training I was called into the coaches' office to meet someone. It was Bill Clark, the new defensive coordinator. Coach Clark was young and he was very intimidating. He looked as though he lived inside a weight room and just the looks he gives is enough to make me want to crawl under a table and hide. They brought Megale, a teammate and middle linebacker, into the meeting with me. Coach Clark told us that he heard a lot about us and that he planned on centering the defense around his middle linebackers. I started to wonder if he was confused—I was an outside linebacker. I didn't know a lot about different defensive schemes but Coach Clark ran a four-three defense where there weren't any outside linebackers in the same way that we had used them in the five-two defense. I had put on a little weight and I was growing because I stayed in the weight room any time I could. My family had moved into the closest house to the football stadium and I made a little gap in the fence behind the concession stand so I could walk to the field house to workout. I had grown to around one hundred-seventy pounds so playing middle linebacker at a large school started to look like a possibility.

Hindsight Joy

Coach Clark told me that he needed me to stay on the weights and pack on some more weight so I could handle the physicality that it would take to play in the middle of the defense. Megale was already built for it and started at linebacker during our sophomore year, which was unheard of at a big school. For some strange reason, I wanted to do whatever Coach Clark told me to do. From the first second I met him, something told me that he would be the greatest influence on me outside of my dad. Coach Clark had a head of thinning hair and the concentration of the remaining hair on his head was at the front, sort of an island of hair. The players had a good time with it—behind his back of course. Of course I had to get in on the fun. One afternoon momma told me that since my dad was bald, I would be too. I didn't believe that at all. I had lot of hair, and I sported the popular 1990's mullet for years. There was no way I would lose it all. Momma said, "Keep making fun of Coach Clark and your baldness will be accelerated". I still didn't think it would happen. Well, it did! By the time I was twenty-four, I had to start planning on how I would make bald look good.

Spring training rolled around and I found myself at the center of the defensive game plan. My respect for Coach Clark grew by the day and I realized that I would do anything to make him like what I was doing on the field. I worked as hard as I could every day during that spring. I no longer had to look across the ball at Dustin, Clay and the behemoths of the past but the new young offensive linemen were aggressive and mean. One of them, of course, was Reggie "Quitty" Plowman, my best friend. We had some violent battles in scrimmages. The other guard on our offense was Wesley, who was my closest friend other than Reggie. They loved when plays were called that required them both to climb to the linebacker and double team me. It was awful! They were so good at it and I still wasn't big enough to handle it. They made me a better player very quickly. I knew that we would never face a team that had the offensive line that we had.

After spring training was over, school ended and the summer workout program started. Coach Clark took over in the weight room and it was intense! I loved it. Some of the guys didn't see it the same way that I did though. I noticed players skipping reps and not doing all their sets and just taking short cuts. It made me pretty mad because I couldn't see how someone could lie to Coach Clark. That all started to change when other players started to see things the same way I did and our team was working harder than ever. It was easy to see that Coach Clark was a great motivator.

Our team started to really bond and we couldn't wait to get the season going. I spent the whole summer staying out of trouble and working out and running. I would do anything extra that could give me an edge on the field. The summer between my sophomore and junior years I gained about twenty-five pounds. I wanted to be two hundred pounds really bad! I got close but just couldn't get over the hump. I wasn't about to quit! I hit the weights even harder in July. In mid July we would getting a max on all of our lifts. This is a day where you see exactly how much you can lift for one repetition and I wanted to do more than anyone else. I loved doing squats and it was my goal to lift more weight on the squat than anyone in the state in my weight class. Coach Clark posted a list of state records on every lift in every weight class. I was one hundred-ninety pounds and the state record on squats in my weight class was five hundred-fifteen pounds. I knew that was in my range and I was going to break that on Max Day.

I worked really hard leading up to Max Day. I was in the weight room at least twice a day working on technique and getting extra help and advice from Coach Clark. On Max Day, I felt great! We started on the flat bench press and I didn't do so well. It never really was my strongest lift; in fact, I bench press more now—at age 41—than I did in high school. Then it was time—time to break a state record! I warmed up with three hundred pounds and my opening lift was four hundred-eighty-five pounds. I lifted that with ease. I then moved up to five hundred-five pounds and that was no problem either. Then, we loaded the bar with five hundred-twenty pounds for the record. I felt great about it. I took the bar, backed into my stance and began to go down to position. As I started back up, my knees started shaking and my right elbow gave out on me. I had issues with my elbow from the terrible break that I had in ninth grade. The bar slammed down on the safety rails and I failed! I was crushed! My elbow was throbbing and locked into an angle. I ended up having to have a minor surgery to repair some cartilage and I had to rehabilitate it quickly because the season was coming. It turned out to be an easy healing and I was ready to go.

Coach Clark's main objective on defense was to get as many of our eleven players around the ball as we could. His desire was having all eleven near the ball when the play was over. From the beginning of summer practice, we ran pursuit drills which conditioned us to be able to get to the football. August Alabama heat is nothing to pay around with. In those days, we didn't have the state athletic association dictating how we practiced, when we could practice or how many practices we could have in one day. We started with two-a-days; one practice in the morning and one in the afternoon, both with full pads on. Nowadays we have to practice three calendar days in shorts and only once a day before we can put pads on. That wasn't the case in 1992.

Every practice ended with the dreaded pursuit drill. We had to sprint, redirect, sprint again and do all of this time after time, with perfection. Coach Clark would settle for nothing less than maximum effort and we were set on giving him that. During one morning practice, we were flying around the field and having fun doing it. We were on board with his all eleven men at the football mentality. It became our goal on every play. No one wanted to be the last guy to the ball so we were competing with each other to make sure we got there first. It was exciting Coach Clark. He wasn't the kind of coach that just stood there with his whistle in his mouth; he was flying around with us. After one rep of pursuit, he yelled, "Gosh almighty, LOOK AT ALL THAT WHITE!"—we wore white jerseys in practice.

That phrase became something we all would say every time we completed a great repetition in pursuit and it is still something my teammates and I say to each other today when we come across each other. I wish words on a page could give you the exact picture and tone in which he said it. We wanted him yelling that phrase all the time; we knew if he was spewing it, we were doing it right. We knew we had a special defense in 1992 and we really believed that we could make a good run at winning a championship.

The season started at Brookwood, a smaller school in the eastern part of Tuscaloosa County. We knew that we would be in for a fight; not in the close game sense, but we knew we would have to fight, literally. The talk all week from their side of the county was that they planned to start a brawl. They had a lot of players that were similar to me in that they liked fighting. I never even considered starting a fight during a game because I was always focused on doing the right thing and trying to win. About half way through the first half, the sky starting lighting up so bright that it looked like afternoon. The lightning was so intense that they sent us inside to let the storm pass.

The storm became worse and it intensified and we went into a tornado warning. We sat in the gym for what seemed like hours; two in fact. We were fortunate enough to escape any great damage around Brookwood's school so we came back out to resume the game. Obviously the crowd had kind of dissipated but it didn't slow down our intensity. The conditions were wet, just like we liked it. Before long, the game got a little 'chippy' and there were several penalties after the whistle on both sides; more on them of course. It looked like when we were just about to put the game away, they starting instituting their plan to start a fight.

It seemed a little bit obvious that every time they had a penalty for something after the play, it was done on their side of the field. Every play they ran was to their sideline when we were on defense. And now it was time to fight. They ran another play to their sideline on the play after I was brought out of the game. At the time, many of us were being taken out because the game was almost in hand. There were still a few starters on the field because we never had to sub too many at one time because we had so much depth. Mike and Barnaby were still out there and this particular play came to their side.

Hindsight Joy

Mike was our defensive end, a tall lanky guy with a lot of meanness in him. He would certainly not be the guy that I would target to start the brawl with, but they did. As we looked across the field, it was obvious that something was going on and I realized that several of their players were surrounding Mike while he was on the ground and were punching and kicking him repeatedly. Barnaby got sucked in and he was next. As all eleven of our players started getting involved, Steve and I grabbed our helmets and started to sprint across the field to help until someone put the brakes on us. Steve is the guy I mentioned during my junior high season that was the best football player I ever knew. He was now about two hundred-twenty-five pounds and strong as a bull. I didn't know anyone that could put the brakes on him.

Until Coach Griffin grabbed both of us by out collars and we couldn't move. Coach Griffin was my position coach for my senior season but at this time, I didn't know him too well. He was a body builder who had won championships with his physique, but he was really short. He may have been vertically challenged, but somehow he had me off the ground by my shoulder pads with one hand and had big Steve in the other hand. There was no way we were getting out of his grip. Our coaches managed to keep most of us from crossing the field and risk getting thrown out of the game and suspended for the next week's game against Gadsden. Mike got roughed up pretty good but they didn't really succeed in beating us in a fight. Their strategy of keeping it on their side of the field was pretty genius. We ended up winning by a few touchdowns but the game didn't end until almost 1:00 am with the tornado delay and the time it took for the referees to sort out who was ejected in the fight.

The next week, we traveled to Gadsden who was nationally ranked and loaded with players that would go on to play at major colleges. I ended up being sick and fever set in while we were on the bus. I tried my best to give it a shot at playing but the coaches decided that I would be better off sitting this one out. It drove me crazy being out of the game. We battled hard but lost a close road game to a great team and it gave us a lot of confidence for the rest of the year. The next week we lost to Selma. It was a game that we should have won. But Selma was really fast and we lost by five.

We split the next two games and were 2-3 going into the part of our schedule that had all three of our area opponents waiting. Our first area game came against Hueytown and we won that game 25-0. Our defense was exactly what we thought we would be. Our offense was starting to get it rolling too. The next week we played West End of Birmingham. This was the biggest team I had ever seen. Their offensive line was full of guys that were over six feet five inches tall and almost 300 pounds. Their size didn't worry us and we went on to win 31-9.

The next week we had our biggest win of the year. Jess Lanier High School was known for being nasty and playing dirty. But they were also really good. We knew we had to win this game to get into the playoffs. The game came right down to the end. They had the ball and were driving with around one minute to play. We were clinging to a 17-14 lead and our grip was slipping. They drove the ball to our 20 yard line and we started to bow up and forced a 4th down and 3 yards to go. We had to get a stop on this play or our chances were not good. They didn't have a good field goal kicker but if they got the first down, he could have a chance.

They ran an option to our right, towards our sideline. My right foot was throbbing and I could feel it swelling up inside my cleats. I wasn't about to tell anyone about it because I wasn't coming out on this fourth down play. As their offense broke the huddle and walked to the line, we got in position and were ready. Behind me was our All-Everything safety, Jason. Jason was a senior and was getting stacks of letters from colleges every day. Every afternoon when he got home from practice, he would walk in his kitchen where a new stack of letters sat. He deserved every one of them; he was a great player. I always knew that if a ball carrier got past us at linebacker, they wouldn't go far because Jason was there.

Jason was barking out orders before the ball was snapped. We both knew that the option play was coming, but I thought they would run it to their sideline, or our left. They snapped the ball and the quarterback stuck the ball in the fullback's gut, but I knew he wasn't giving it to him. He pulled it and went RIGHT! I had only guessed half right. I redirected and started toward the quarterback when he got his read and pitched it to the running back. I changed my angle and just when I made contact with the ball carrier Jason knocked me out of the way and finished the play. We looked at the chains across the field and realized that we had stopped him short and we would win the game!

The game ended just like our pursuit drills; we competed with each other to get to the ball as much as we competed with our opponents. I got credit for half a tackle on that play, but I know that Jason wouldn't have got to him if I hadn't made first contact and I also know that he may have fallen forward for a first down if Jason hadn't finished him off. It was team competition and team work all at the same time.

The next week we played a non-region game against Anniston. Anniston was undefeated and ranked #3 in the state and they were scoring a lot of points and giving up few. This game was really important simply because every game is, but the following week, we would enter Bryant-Denney Stadium and play our rival, the Central Falcons. It was important that we didn't lose focus on Anniston which would be really easy to do. But it's really hard to look past a team as good as Anniston. We prepared all week without even thinking about our finale with Central and we played well staying close until the end, losing 21-10. After the game, Coach Clark walked up to me in the locker room and said I played well, the whole defense did. He then informed me that for the Central game, he had a different plan for me and we would discuss it Sunday when we came in to watch film.

The anticipation for Sunday killed me all night Friday and all day Saturday. I had no idea what I was in for, but I trusted Coach Clark and I knew that he was more than capable of putting me wherever I needed to be to help the team. Sunday came and I walked into the film room a nervous wreck. We watched the film of the Anniston game and talked about how to correct what we did wrong and I still didn't know what this plan was for me. My stomach started hurting as I anxiously waited for the news. I wasn't so much worried as I was excited! I just wanted to be a part of the plan no matter in what capacity.

Coach Clark put on Central's film from their game against Greenwood High School from Mississippi. Central had a new coach that year, Coach Busby and he was a genius at the old school wishbone offense. Their offense was huge and their backs were really good. Their whole plan is to run the ball, over and over again while trying to get the defense tired. The old saying 'three yards and a cloud of dust' was very sufficient in describing what they liked to do, and they did it well. I was still just around one hundred-ninety pounds and every player on their offense, including the backs, was heavier than I was. I wasn't sure if Coach Clark was going to put me in the secondary and have me play run support or move me outside and put a bigger player in the middle. I didn't care, I just wanted to know!

After watched about a half of that film, Coach Clark changed the film and we began watching Central's game with Parker High School. Their offense was dominating and driving Parker's big defensive linemen off the ball at will—except for one. He was smaller than the rest and he was almost untouched coming through the line and he had to blocked by a back because the line couldn't get a hand on him. Coach Clark looked at me and said, "Brehm, you will be playing the 'one-technique' this week. But instead of getting blocked by the back, you will cause problems and change their angles." (The one-technique is on the inside shoulder of the offensive guard and right in the middle of all of those big bodies)

I didn't question him, I never did, and I simply agreed as if I had a choice in the matter. He said he heard I could get off the ball really quick from my days as a fullback and he thought I would be perfect for this assignment. After the film session, I went out to the football field and spent a couple of hours working on a good defensive lineman stance and getting off the ball as fast as I could. I didn't want to wait until practice to be able to do these things. I was used to standing up when the ball was snapped so this was going to be really different for me.

We installed the game plan that week and it was time to cross the Hugh Thomas Bridge into Tuscaloosa and try to defeat Central for the first time in four years. We knew it wouldn't be easy. They had beaten us pretty bad in the last two meetings. The two years before that, both games were close. We had to show that we had improved and we needed to do it early in the game. If Central gets a lead on an opponent, they use their style of offense to wear teams down while using as much clock as they could.

I was adjusting to my new role pretty well and I was doing what I was supposed to do and the defense was playing great. We battled the whole game in front of over twenty thousand fans in the cold air but we fell short and lost 22-10 as Central pulled away late in the game. We were 5-5 and missed the playoffs due to tiebreakers after finishing tied for first place in the area. It was tough to see our seniors not get a chance to play on, but we knew we needed to get right back to work for the next season. When we got back to the school, Coach Clark called me over and asked, "How'd you like playing in the trenches with your hand in the dirt?" Of course my answer was that I loved it! "Good, you'll be there all year next season!"

Chapter Eleven

From Dallas to Decisions

For the rest of the winter I couldn't stop thinking about how bad it felt seeing my senior teammates play their last game. It was gut-wrenching and it was magnified by the thought that I only had one season left and it was fast approaching. I thought about my new position and what I needed to do to get better. I couldn't help but worry about how I would hold up over a ten-week season being smaller than the typical big school defensive lineman. I felt like I needed to gain some weight and I wasn't sure how I would accomplish that given the fact that I ate like a race horse and never gained an ounce.

I had talks with Coach Clark leading up to Spring Training about how I could prepare my body for the beating I would take in the trenches. His advice was, get stronger and get faster at the snap of the ball. He told me that weight gain wasn't important. The memory of missing the state record on the squat lift crept back in my mind and I knew that chasing that record would motivate me and I would get stronger in the process. I immediately started to work on my strength especially in that lift. I realized that I was really close to the state record in the power cling as well. The power cling is a full-body lift where explosion is the key to getting the bar off the ground and to your upper chest in a hurry. The record in the one hundred-ninety-pound class was 345 pounds and I had done around 325 pounds in the past.

Suddenly two records were in my reach and I went to work to achieve both. That summer my mom's brother, Uncle Richard, called me and asked me to come out to his house in Wolfe City, Texas because some of the Dallas Cowboys were having a full pad camp at East Texas State University, now known as Texas A&M-Commerce. Pop and Nana had been huge Cowboys fans my entire life and I was excited to work with a few of them. Jay Novacek, the All-Pro Tight End was the director of the camp and my favorite player, linebacker Ken Norton, Jr would be a coach. Nana and I drove to Texas and instead of staying on campus for the camp, I drove Uncle Richard's farm truck to and from practice; about a fifteen mile drive one way.

There were several college coaches there helping and recruiting but I hadn't really thought about the recruiting process because I was still undersized for my position and I didn't think playing in college was a possibility. The first day, we did things like the forty-yard dash, bench press reps and some agility testing. I ran the fastest forty-yard dash time I had ever run; 4.58 seconds. Coach Spillman from East Central Community College in Mississippi walked over to me and handed me his business card and said he wanted to see me at middle linebacker the next day when we would start practicing in pads. It was just fine with me since that's what I had been playing for the last year. A couple of other coaches talked with me that evening and some were very interested and some said they wished I was three inches taller and twenty pounds heavier.

There were over one hundred-fifty high school players at this camp and there were some really good players. I was a little worried about how I would do with the level of competition. As we started our first practice, I settled in pretty well and during the individual drills, I stood out from the other linebackers. Coach Spillman stayed with my group watching me for the whole first day. After a couple of days of practice, they divided us up into two teams and we started to prepare for a game that we would play against each other on the last day of camp. Of course I wanted to win that game, but I wanted to be selected in the camp's Top 30 Club and be the defensive MVP.

That camp was so much fun and it allowed me to realize that playing in college was a real possibility. The day before the game, we learned different workout routines for all body parts and new techniques on running the "forty". Since I had clocked such a good time on the first day, I started trash talking Jay Novacek. Jay was the best tight end in the National Football League. He was really tall and didn't look like he was very fast. He talked about his relationship with Christ throughout the whole week and gave us a lot of stories to help us grow up as men and stressed the importance of salvation through Jesus. Jay was humble in his success and drove a modest truck and you could never tell that he was a wealthy professional athlete.

Because I kept talking trash to him about his speed, he challenged me to a race. I didn't blink an eye and went straight to the starting line continuing my trash talk. I didn't think this lanky tight end could run with me. I was very, very wrong. When we were given the start command, all I saw was his back and he grew smaller as he ran away from me. I guess I could've been embarrassed, but he was the best at what he did and I was the only one with the courage to race him in front of all the campers and a stadium full of spectators. I lost, but to a famous professional football player.

Game day was here! I was so excited to put into practice the things I learned throughout the week. They wouldn't let us wear our football pants— we wore shorts—because they didn't want us going to the ground on tackles for injury sake. They put flags on our belts and we were supposed grab the flag in lieu of tackling the ball carrier. I only knew one speed and it was FAST! I just couldn't get the message from my brain to my body to grab the flag instead of tackle the runner. Tackling was a penalty in this game and I got penalized at least a half dozen times before it registered that I needed to grab the flag. I had a great game and now it was time for awards.

We all sat on the field sweaty and tired as Jay addressed the parents and spectators. He began naming the 'Top 30 Club' and the nerves started to get rough on my stomach; I wanted that T-Shirt and that title! He called my name pointing out that I was one of the hardest working high school players he ever saw and the most penalized as well. I was content with being in the club and as the contentment set in, I was announced as the camp defensive most valuable player. I couldn't believe that out of over 150 players from all over the country, I was noticed as the best. I was one of the last campers to leave the stadium because I was stopped and talked to by at least eight college coaches from all over the nation. It was overwhelming, but now I knew that if I worked hard and God allowed me to grow an inch or two, I could play football in college.

I made the decision on the way back to Alabama that no one would outwork me. There were a couple of weeks before summer workouts started so I had time to get a head start on my teammates. The workouts that we learned at camp were all eight minute workouts and I did every one of them, everyday. I didn't give my body much rest. I wanted to be ahead of the rest of my teammates when they reported and I wanted to start getting ready to set the state squat and power clean record. The size of my legs started to accelerate and my upper body wasn't quite catching up. But I was getting stronger every day. To begin our summer training program, we always started with a Max Day to set what percentages we would lift during our workouts and I wanted to match the state records on that day.

The day the team reported, we had a few meetings and then warmed up to get maxes. I was warming up with much more weight than what most of my teammates maxed at. My goal was five hundred-forty pounds on the squat and a power clean of three hundred-forty. I was successful on both lifts. It was a great summer as my teammates and I got stronger and we began to take great pride in working hard. The upcoming season seemed to be looking bright for us and it was rapidly approaching. Through it all, I couldn't stop thinking about playing in college. I started receiving letters from coaches every now and then, not nearly to the level that Jason was the year before, but every one was a huge deal to me, especially the ones from Coach Chan Gailey who had been a head coach in the NFL and at major colleges. I still have a couple of his letters today. Before our season began, I had several college visits set up for the season and I was looking forward to going to all of them.

Heath was a friend that really loved Jesus. He was raised in a Christian home and his parents, Wade and Patsy were known around the neighborhood as loving people that cared about the well-being of everyone, especially the kids. At the time, I had cut myself odd from everything that involved the church, Jesus or anyone that wanted to talk about it. I was at a time in my life that I relied on myself and my abilities and I was putting football above everything, especially the relationship with Christ that I had forgotten. Heath was the one friend that I had that cared more about my eternity than my talents. When I did go to a youth event or just to a church service, it was with him and his family. I had convinced myself that this "sunscreen faith" that I was practicing was enough and I didn't need any of the day to day reliance of a Savior. I was good without it.

I got a little bit of attention going into my senior season and I never gave any credit to God for the things He had been enabling me to do. Coach Clark regularly talked about having a platform as a football player in our city to make an impact on people. He stressed to me the importance of using my influence as a player to show Jesus in my life. Again, his words went in one ear and out the other. I felt like I was all I needed and football was my passion. Most of what I ignored in my teenage years would end up being the same thing I stressed to players later on in my coaching career and I wish I knew then what I know now. I sit and wonder how different it would've been then if I had a deep passion for Jesus and coupled that passion with my passion to be the best football player that I could be. I have some regret about that since now I know how impactful "platform and influence" can be and how it can help people see Jesus.

I watched football on TV every weekend and I heard athletes give credit for their talents and abilities to God. Even in hearing that, I still never let it creep in my mind that God did indeed give me the drive that I needed to be as good as I could be. I thought that if God had anything to do with my ability, He would've given me the size I needed to get even more attention. In hindsight, I understand that He gave me the determination, the drive, the desire, the motor and the strength as an undersized player so that I could use those traits to benefit others as I grew up and started my career. It is funny the things you see in hindsight even those things that have been removed from your life. I could have gone into my senior season with a motivation to show Christ in my life through the platform He gave me, but instead, I began that season selfishly seeking ways to enhance the attention I got and I worried about reputation and not my platform. And it almost all went the way that I had wanted it to.

Chapter Twelve

The One Man Wrecking Crew

The summer of 1993 was tough. The team worked really hard to get ready to be successful. We had lost a lot of great players due to graduation after the 1992 season and we had so many holes to fill just to remain competitive. I knew that we had better not let any ball carriers get past us up front because Jason was gone playing in college. We returned some great players too, and the sophomore class had several guys that we knew could contribute and step into some key spots on offense and defense. There was no question that we were ready to play. Our weight room had turned into a battle ground where we all competed with each other to see who could show the most gains in strength. It was a good thing because every one of us, all one hundred of us, got stronger and faster.

The schedule was going to be the same as the year before, but we would just change the game site. The schedule for the 1993 season was loaded with top ten teams but we were set to start with Brookwood, this time at home and under better weather conditions. Both teams were on probation due to the altercation the year before. All this meant was that if it happened again, we would receive a bigger punishment. I was wondering if Brookwood even cared about that. I was ready for the same thing to happen and for them to start an even bigger fight. I had my mind made up that this year, I wouldn't be held back if it happened.

Trying to get the thought of a fight was tough to do. We knew we had a job to do, but getting past what happened in 1992 was difficult. This would be my first game as a defensive lineman. Over the summer, we installed a new defensive scheme that would allow me to get deep in the backfield and create problems for the quarterback even if he was just handing the ball off. I wasn't real certain how this would work for me. Brookwood had some really big offensive linemen and I weighed less than two-hundred pounds. I would have to use my quickness when the ball was snapped in order to be effective.

It was game time and time to show how hard we had worked since November after losing the last game of the year to Central. It didn't take long for our defense to start dominating. I made two tackles behind the line of scrimmage on the first possession. The second possession was much the same as I had begun to play the best game of my life. I just knew that they would make some adjustments to take me out of the game either in some type of dirty playing tactics or run the other way. Running the other way didn't work either. Big Terry, all three hundred pounds of him played on the left side and he took up a lot of space. By the time the running back decided which way to maneuver around the space Terry took up, I was there making the tackle. Megale and the other linebackers were playing great too. They were stopping plays that got past the linemen and redirecting Brookwood's runners and I was piling up the statistics.

At halftime, the joke in the locker-room was who would tackle me in order for someone else to get some tackles on Brookwood runners. I was in such a zone that the same thing was happening in the second half. We were playing great assignment defense and I was making all the tackles. I was getting a lot of credit, but on a field that is over fifty yards wide, the other ten guys had to be doing their jobs well in order for me to do what I was doing. I ended up with six quarterback sacks, five tackles for loss and was in on several other tackles. I forced a few fumbles too. The Tuscaloosa News reporter that covered our game called me the "One-Man Wrecking Crew" in the article for the Saturday paper. I wasn't real pleased with that because we played great as a defense and won the game 25-0. I didn't want to be singled out and that fact was kind of foreign to me because I was usually all about myself. But I remembered years earlier, the quote "Don't I always" and I didn't want that to be me.

That was a great night nonetheless. We won a game with a local rival, the weather was good and we didn't have to fight to get out of there. It was great starting point for our season. We still had work to do because week after week, we would be playing great teams and week two was the beginning of that. Gadsden High School was coming to town and they were nationally ranked and loaded with Division 1 football players just like the year before. I was a team captain for the game and I couldn't wait to walk out there in front of the home crowd for the coin toss. We felt pretty good about being able to win the game.

This game was a battle from the kickoff until the end of the over time that it took for Gadsden to beat us 28-21. A late fumble and yet another one during overtime was the difference in the game, but we couldn't be upset about the way played on defense or on offense. I had a tough game that week as they double teamed me all night which was expected. But my team mates took up the slack and did what they were supposed to do when one guy draws a double team. We were so well-coached that we knew how to handle it. A lucky bounce here or there during that game and the result would've been different, but we had a lot to be happy about and reason to have a positive outlook for the rest of the season.

The next week we were playing a really fast Selma High School team with an incredible wide receiver who we had to stop in order to win. This guy was tall, fast and could jump higher than anyone I've ever seen. When watching film, we noticed that he was 'over-the-top' arrogant and he really annoyed us. Every time he made a good play, he would spring away from everyone else, come to a sudden stop and pose to the opposing sideline with his hands on his hips. He was all about himself and didn't appear to care very much about his team. But we knew we had to find ways to keep the quarterback from getting him that ball and we would have to do that by keeping him from even getting a pass off. We did what we had planned to do and won the game 26-13.

The fourth week of the season came really quick. We had to travel a little bit north to play Fayette County, a smaller school with a lot of great players. The quarterback was a state record holder in almost every passing category there was. He eventually went on to play at Alabama and his favorite receiver played for the Atlanta Braves. We were the favorites to win the game but we knew this would be a tough game to win in the manner that we should have. We were getting one of our best linebackers back for the first time that season and it came at the right time.

The weather was hot and humid. It was almost impossible to breathe without feeling like your lungs were filling up with water. The mosquitoes were out of control and I was getting chewed up! My arms and neck were red and full of bumps from the onslaught from the vicious bugs. It was obvious that we were all bothered by them. The Fayette Tigers seemed unbothered as if they were just accustomed to the attacks. I can't say that the mosquito invasion was the reason we didn't play so well, but it definitely affected the way that I performed. I had what was by far the worst game of my high school career. I was used to playing against offensive linemen that were much bigger than I was, but this particular game was different. The guy lined up across from me was about thirty pounds lighter than me and I couldn't get by him. My quickness off the ball was no longer an advantage because this guy was equally as fast. I couldn't wait to just get this game over! The linebacker, Mark, that was playing for the first time that year intercepted a pass late in the game and sealed the victory, 14-13.

One of my favorite memories of playing in high school was the long bus trips, particularly the ones that we took on charter buses. Those trips made us feel like college players and the feeling of importance and celebrity was magnified just by the bus we boarded. Our week five opponent was the number four team in the state, Enterprise High School. They too were the Wildcats and every reporter in the state thought we had little to no chance of competing in that game. Enterprise was about four hours away and the long bus trip would likely have a negative impact on the way we played the game and they had one of the top ranked offensive linemen, the top ranked linebacker and the best running back in the state. We knew we had our hands full.

We boarded the bus midmorning and headed south as a heavy underdog. The pride I felt as I walked up the steps of that bus was really memorable. I was wondering if this was the feeling that I could get every time I played on the road in college. The thought of playing in college was still strong in my mind and I was confident that I would make it. As we got to rolling down the highway, I got a pinch of snuff, my first and toughest addiction I have ever had. As a high school football player with no part time job, I had to be selective about the snuff that I bought. All I had on that road trip was the cheapest snuff offered, and it was whiskey flavored. It was terrible! Unfortunately, I fell asleep with a mouth full of it.

We were scheduled to stop at Troy State University, about forty-five minutes north of Enterprise, to have a walk through practice on their football team's practice field. My sister, Jackie, was a sophomore majorette there and it was pretty exciting to go there with my team and walk around on the field that my sister performed on at every home game. I had slept for almost the entire trip to Troy, with that mouth full of whiskey-flavored snuff. As I walked off the bus, I hurriedly spit it out and spent the entire practice chewing gum, drinking water and Gatorade trying everything I could to get that taste out of my mouth. NOTHING worked. I ended up having a hint of the whiskey flavor on my mouthpiece for the next two weeks and I never would buy that stuff again!

We had finally arrived in Enterprise, Alabama and settled into the visitor's locker room and recovered from the long bus ride. As the usual nerves set in, we had our pregame team meetings and got ready to go play as a heavy underdog. The stadium was massive, and the home side was almost filled to capacity an hour prior to the kickoff. As we exited the locker room to begin pregame warm ups, we had to actually walk down the steps, through the sea of Enterprise fans and onto the field at the north end zone. Their fans let us know that they were there, rudely. We didn't really worry about what was being said to us and we surely weren't intimidated at all. Rowdy fans are common in Alabama so it wasn't out of the ordinary and it wasn't too tasteless, it was just part of big high school football in our state. After pregame warm ups, we had to walk back up those same steps, through that same sea of fans. The only part we didn't like was how far the walk was and how many steps we had to climb in our football cleats.

It was time to come out for the coin toss and there we go again, down those same steps and this time the seats were packed with even more rowdy football fans. I could see how that could be a factor in the way the visiting team would play, but not us. We were zoned in from the time we got on the bus that morning. We knew we had to be at our very best on defense to stop this offense. Their running back was much bigger than I was and he was committed to play at the University of Tennessee. This game would be much different from the week before because the offensive line was a lot bigger than Fayette County's. How would we stop this huge offensive machine from scoring at will on us? The key had always been, follow Coach Clark's game plan, and play as hard as we can and do the fundamentals and not miss tackles. We were sure that we would be just fine.

As the game went on, we kept stopping them and our offense kept the ball and chewed up big minutes off of the clock. The game plan was being executed almost perfectly. At halftime we had a small lead and Enterprise's huge offense had not advanced the ball past the fifty-yard line yet. We had shut them out for an entire half. And there we went up those same steps into the locker room for halftime. It was really tiring having those big guys push us around and us pushing back and then having to take that long walk to the locker room knowing we had to come back down when the second half began. The fans were still loud and obnoxious, but never said anything offensive or vulgar; just normal stuff.

The second half was equally as tough and as we got more tired, it became more difficult to push back. Anyone who has any knowledge of football could have thought that eventually their offense would wear us down with their size and speed and take the lead. That never happened. I was battling cramps in my calf muscles the entire second half. It was hard to put my foot on the ground much less run and keep those linemen from driving me through the turf. But late in the fourth quarter with the clock ticking away, we realized that their offense still had only advanced the ball across the fifty yard-line one time and we were dominating the game. The offense continued to keep the ball for big chunks of time and we won the game 16-0. We had pulled off an incredible upset hours away from home. As I ran onto the field as the clock read zeroes, the cramps overtook me and I couldn't move. I fell to the ground for a brief moment when Coach Moore yelled at me to get up and stop showing weakness after a big victory. I just couldn't lie there anymore and sprung to my feet to join the celebration. But how would I get back up those steps and how would that bus ride home be? It all worked out. It is amazing what you can get your body to do if you win.

Our first area game, which was the first game that counted towards gaining a playoff spot, was the next week. Our opponent was Hueytown and we were on the road again. We were overwhelming favorites to win this game, but after the battle and long trip we had the previous week, we were primed for a huge letdown. I had a good game, making several tackles, forcing a couple of fumbles and recovering one. We won easily, 26-14, but it wasn't up to the standards that Coach Moore and Coach Clark had for us and they weren't happy. It was a strange feeling on the bus as we were told that we would be practicing on that Sunday afternoon because we had two very tough opponents for the next couple of weeks and we had a lot to improve on.

West End of Birmingham was undefeated and climbing rankings. They were still as big as the year before and maybe even stronger. Their offensive line looked like tall trees on film. The offensive lineman that I would be up against was at least six-foot-nine inches tall and mean. I could tell that he was a really dirty player but I wasn't scared of him and planned to fight dirty play with quickness. He appeared to be a guy that if he got aggravated, he would eventually give up. It didn't go quite as I though it would. I had a decent game and we fought until the end losing 21-7. Their defense was great and had only given up 20 points on the year, and our offense gave them about all they could handle, time just ran out on us. West End would go on that year and play for the 6A Class State Championship, they were just that good.

Jess Lanier High was next and they were looking to avenge the loss we handed them in 1992. This time, we would visit Snitz Snider Memorial Stadium in Bessemer, their home. This stadium was famous for being intimidating and just plain scary. Opposing teams have had their bus nearly tipped over, things thrown at the windows and anything else you could think of that would strike fear in the minds of the visitors. Most schools wouldn't even allow their school bands to even attend games played at Snitz Snider, but ours did. We fumbled the opening kickoff and they got on the scoreboard first. We played pretty good for the entire game. Our offense was keeping the ball for chunks of minutes and our defense was stopping them from mounting long drives and scoring on quick plays like they were accustomed to doing.

Just before halftime, our band was to our left warming up for their halftime performance. They were on the end of the field that was parallel to the main road through that part of town. Gunshots began out on the street and the whole band hit the ground. The majority of our team was so focused on what was going on within the game that we just stood there—with the exception of big Terry who joined the band face down on the ground. It has been topic of comedy with Terry ever since. We were tied late and we forced a punt. We were sure that this would be our chance to score and end the game. We fumbled the punt and Jess Lanier scored moments later and we lost a hard fought battle 21-14. Now we had to get changed quickly and get on the bus and on our way in a hurry. We got on the road with no issues and no one was hurt—during our exit OR the shooting.

Anniston was a great team with the best quarterback in the state. He was very big to be a quarterback and he was committed to play at Alabama. It was going to be a huge test and we were looking forward to it. As the weather forecast for that Friday started to be released, it appeared that this game would be a wet one. Weather forecasts in the early 1990's were much different and less reliable than they are today, so we held out hope that it wouldn't be too bad. But I was hoping for torrential rains because it would slow down Anniston's passing attack. Either way, we had to prepare for a dry field as well as a wet one.

It turns out that the rain that night would be historical. It was pouring all day. As we reported to the field house to get ready, the field—at least the sidelines—was covered in many inches of water. You couldn't even see the lines on the field. And the rain never stopped and only slowed down for a few minutes at a time. As the game started, we felt like the rain would benefit us as a defense and would definitely assist our offenses run-heavy game plan. It turned out to be the case as our offense kept the ball for much of the game and our defense held them to only seven points on the night. On one of the most memorable plays in my high school career, I ran the quarterback out of the pocket and he headed towards their sideline to try and get rid of the ball. I tackled him out of bounds and when we went to the ground, I realized that we were both in about six inches of water. We won that game 21-7 and had pulled of our second big upset of a highly ranked team on the season. I didn't get out of that game without a battle wound though. As I was making their big tackle angry, he went inside my facemask and inserted his huge finger into my eye socket. It had to be his entire finger. My eye swelled closed and turned a different shade of blue. I was proud of my discolored eye—a win will make a lot of things worth it.

Chapter Thirteen

Welcome to the Big Leagues, Big Boy

Reggie and I had a lot of close friends at Central Tuscaloosa High School. In fact, we spent the majority of our free time hanging out and running the roads with Shawn, Courtney, Mark, Curry and Greg—all players at Central, our next opponent and biggest rival. This rivalry was, in our opinion, the absolute biggest football rivalry in the state and they had recently 'owned' us. We hadn't beaten them since 1988 and most years it wasn't even a close game, except the year before. We rarely talked about the rivalry in our group of friends throughout the year. They didn't taunt Reggie and me the year before and there was little trash talk leading up to the game in 1993. There were other friends of ours that we weren't as close to that had a little bit to say, Marty in particular.

Marty was Central's big fullback. They ran the old school wishbone offense and he was in the middle of it all, and he was really good. He taunted me in the days leading up to the game but it was all in fun. I always liked Marty, and I still do. But I knew that for those forty-eight minutes, we would hate each other and that's how it was supposed to be. Greg was their center and the head coach's son, Courtney was their guard, Curry was the other guard and Shawn was their huge tackle. I knew it would be really strange lining up across from four of my closest friends. Mark played on the defense along with a few of our other buddies so it would be strange to Reggie as well. The anticipation was tense, but we all had fun with it anyway.

Hindsight Joy

Our group of friends did everything together. It was interesting how we all ended up becoming friends. One weekend during our junior year, Reggie and I were just riding around looking for something to do and we ended up pulling into a burger place because there were a whole bunch of cars and trucks there and they were all being loaded up with people, at the same time. We just knew there was about to be a caravan of cars headed to a party, so we just jumped in line. With the rivalry between the schools, it wouldn't have been out of the question that we would have a hard time staying away from a fight, but they were cool guys and that night, we found lifelong friends in a much unexpected way.

Most weekends we would all start at the burger place. The parking lot would be full of kids from Central, Tuscaloosa Academy, the local private school, and me and Reggie, the lone ones from County High. When we were all together, the schools we attended never mattered, having fun and friendship did. I have so many memories with all of those guys, as a group and individually. Mark was the quiet one. He wasn't one to shy away from confrontation though. To mistake his quietness with weakness would be a great mistake. He was the only one that never did any drinking and I did less than everyone else, though there were those nights that I did. Mark and I had different ways to toe the line of getting in trouble. Some nights when everyone else were on dates or doing something we didn't feel like doing, we would load a cooler with fruit punch bottles and small bottles of milk and put it in the back of his little Ford Ranger pick up truck. He would drive around until we found a police officer that we could purposely get in front of while driving down the road. Then, after we got in front, I would slide open the back window and reach into the cooler and grab a milk or a juice just to spark the curiosity of the officer. We got stopped a couple of times and got a laugh out of one officer. Another didn't see it as being too funny and scolded me for not wearing a seatbelt.

Courtney was the life of the party and you could tell that from the moment he walked in a room. He was always the one that we had to worry

77

about losing. He would act on a moment without much thought to consequences and a lot of times, it created chaos, but I loved the guy. He was usually the guy that made the weekend's plans for everything and we all would follow whatever he planned. Shawn was a huge guy, about six-foot-six. He was really good in school and was normally the one that would either pull us out of trouble, or keep us out of it altogether. Curry was the comedian. At times, there would be a tense situation that needed some inserted humor and he would deliver. Curry became a fire fighter and he recently passed away after having a heart attack. His funeral was one of the toughest events that I had ever been to. Greg was a tough guy. He was short and thick and could throw his weight around at will. Greg was your typical coach's son and knew a lot about football.

On a typical weekend night, we would eventually get ran off from the burger place by the cops and we would move to a local elementary school where there was a straightaway in the street out front that led to a very little used road. We would often line that straightaway with cars and trucks and just hang out until the same officers came to relocate us yet again. From there, we'd move to the local ball park and utilize that parking lot as a party location. That cycle would repeat a couple of times a night until curfew came close and everyone started to head home. We were a tight-knit group of friends, but the big game was coming up!

The Central vs. County High rivalry was huge in our county. Central was the inner city school and was a traditional powerhouse program with numerous state titles. We were the largest county school trying to find an identity. Only three miles separated our campuses but the Black Warrior River made it take a little longer to get from one campus to the other. The bridge over the river is a six-lane state highway and usually loaded with traffic. Running parallel to the state bridge was a railroad bridge and the side of the bridge was highly visible from the highway. Every year, each school's students would brave the dangers of walking out on that rail bridge to hang a sign facing the highway that would exclaim its school pride and usually contained some type of derogatory phrase directed towards the rival. The dangers were obvious—if a train came, you had better be able to run as fast as you can over rail road tracks or have a firm grip on the side of the bridge if you had to jump or hang off until the train passed. It was a prideful event when it was successful. On game day, students would litter the bridge with decorations and the colors of those decorations would change from one side of the river to the other.

None of the rivalry week antics were distasteful on most years. In 1987—I may be off a year—students from Central set a small bomb off on the front steps of our school and blew the doors off. That was the most extreme prank that I can remember. Today, the Central-County rivalry has ended due to new city schools being built and creating three smaller schools and County high grew. The two schools rarely play each other anymore. Today's rivalries have become a contest to see what school can vandalize the other the most or who can hang the biggest, most vulgar sign on the other school. It is less about the game, and more about who can be the most criminal group. I could go on for days about how much disdain I have for things like Homecoming, senior day and all of the other things in high school sports that have been introduced which create distractions for the athletes. Homecoming in my new hometown is a week long crime spree of unneeded toilet paper throwing, kidnapping and fake fighting. I am usually the most hated man in town on that week because I don't hide from my hatred for the events. I'm always told that its all in good fun but the only good fun that I crave is winning!

Winning hadn't come very often for us against Central. We had inched closer in the last couple of years and fell just a touchdown short in 1992. In that game, I had begun my new position at defensive line and I had loved playing there all year, and had done pretty well. As preparations began for the big game, I was once again called into the coach's office much like the year before. I didn't have any clue what this meeting was about but I knew there had to be a different plan for me in this game. When I walked in, Coach Clark wasn't there yet so I sat there with knots in my stomach wondering what this was about. Coach Moore just sat there and smiled at me telling me

79

that I would be okay and there was no need to worry. Coach Moore was always smiling, and sometimes, his smile meant you were in trouble. You couldn't really read him from the expression on his face. It was painful because we always knew that we had to wait for him to speak to know exactly what the current facial expression actually meant.

That smile ended up being a good smile. Coach Clark walked in and said, "Brehm, we have a plan for you this week that is probably not anything you or anyone else has ever seen before. You're going to play a 'flex-nose' position." He was right, I had never heard of anything like this before but I was thrilled that he thought that I could pull off a position that up to this point had never existed—at least to my knowledge. That was all he told me about it at the time. Going in to film session on Monday morning, I still had little clue what this 'flex-nose' position was but it sounded like it would be in the middle of the defense and that was quite scary and exciting all at the same time. In Central's wishbone offense, you have to find a way to stop their charge in the middle. And that was NOT going to be easy to do.

Central's offense was eleven huge humans and their running backs were big too. Across the offensive line, they had all of my buddies and Shawn went on to start at Vanderbilt for most of his time there. Greg played somewhere in Arkansas and their tight end went on to Houston. The quarterback, DeAnthony played for Arkansas, Marty went on to Ole Miss, Dennis, one of the tail backs went to Alabama and for a while, he was the all time leading rusher for the Crimson Tide, and Freddie went on to play at Auburn. Imagine being under two-hundred pounds and being told that you will be put in a position that will be the focal point and the key to stopping all of that Division 1 College football talent. That was the situation I was in the more I learned about this new assignment. For the first time in my football life, I was genuinely scared—or at least a little nervous.

My new position would be lined up directly on Greg, the center, at about two yards deep, and squatted lower than a regular linebacker but with my hands off the ground. I was told to go wherever Marty went and attack the lead blockers and if I could make a tackle, make it, but my job was to disrupt the blockers from getting to our linebackers. I knew this would be a very very violent night and Marty and I would have a long night trying to destroy each other. I had to be ready for his trash talk and his aggressiveness too and try to keep my cool and remember that after it was all over, we were still friends. But for forty-eight minutes, I hated Marty and he hated me even more.

The night was cold and wet. The rain was coming in sideways, a misting rain unlike the rain the week before when it seemed to be coming up from the ground. Neither team threw the ball very much so the rain didn't benefit either of us; it was just a nuisance. It didn't rain the whole night, just enough to make us cold and uncomfortable. One side of Bryant-Denney stadium was nearly packed; red on one side and our Wildcat blue on the other with numerous law enforcement officials between them. Recently, the stadium workers had placed a small chain-link fence between the fans to assist the police if an altercation ensued. It was usually peaceful, but you just never know.

Each year, we traded sidelines and this was the year that the fans would be behind us on our sidelines. The atmosphere was fantastic! There was different feel to it during pregame but the knots in my stomach were intense. I knew I had an uncommon job to do and it would take an extremely uncommon performance to pull it off. When we went into the home locker room after pregame warmups, we were confident that we were ready. Our coaches had us prepared as well a team could be prepared. Now it was really up to us to make it all work. The offense needed to keep that ball away from their offense and our defense had to minimize the amount of yards that their huge offense was used to rolling up. Central was the number six team in the state and their only in state loss came to Robert E. Lee of Montgomery who was the number one team the entire year and ranked in the top five nationally. That score was 24-21. We knew that we had to play the game of our lives to even come close to winning.

After the coin flip, we would be receiving the opening kickoff and I told Reggie as the offense trotted on the field to make sure they keep the ball for as long as they can. The more clock our offense could take away, the better our chances to slow that offensive machine. Reggie and the offense, led by our quarterback, Brent, mounted a touchdown drive that took over eight minutes off of the clock. It was the perfect start. We couldn't have scripted a better beginning to it. The only problem was, it had been over an hour since pregame warmups and the defense had sat on the sidelines for a long time in the cold misting rain. But we couldn't let the elements stop us because we knew that their offense didn't care how cold it was, they were coming out to kill us.

After the kickoff, I trotted onto the field knowing that the alignment that we would be in would surprise everyone. It was a gamble that we were taking to do something like this, but as always, we trusted Coach Clark's game plan. All of my buddies and their huge team mates broke the huddle and sprinted to the ball. Greg grabbed the ball and I squatted into my unfamiliar position. Central's offense could not have cared any less what alignment we were in because they were going to do what they do and run it right at us. Greg snapped the ball to DeAnthony and handed it off to Dennis behind Marty and Freddie. There was over six-hundred pounds of big time football talent coming through the same hole and most of the time, defenses could do very little to stop it.

I sort of made a small misstep on that first play and Marty beat me through the hole. But it allowed me to slip underneath the block and meet Dennis in the air as he jumped over the huge pile of man that our defense created. It was one of the most memorable tackles of my life and it set the tone for the rest of the game. Somehow, even though Dennis and I met at the top of that pile, I ended up at the bottom and felt a tugging and twisting on my foot and ankle. Someone was wrenching my foot like they were trying to snap it off. I looked down to my foot as the bodies began to get off of me and there he was, my buddy Marty, twisting and laughing. When we caught eye contact, he yelled at me, "Welcome to the big leagues, big boy!" He was right, I was now in the big leagues, playing a great football team loaded with talent, in front of over twenty-thousand fans and I was focal point of our efforts to slow them down.

Most of the first half was pretty much the same. We would mount long drives, sometimes gaining very little in terms of yardage, but taking chunks of time off of the clock and our defense would manage to stop them and get off the field. After one of our offensive possessions, we punted to them and Dennis took it to the house for a touchdown. After one of our touchdowns, Dameion, a backup running back that would have been the star player on any other team, outran everyone on our kickoff team for a touchdown. Our defense did give up one score to their offense and we fell behind 21-14 late in the game.

We managed another stop late in the fourth quarter and got the ball back for our offense with one last chance to win the game. After managing the clock for the whole game, our offense was now in a position where they had to move a little quicker. That was troubling because our offense wasn't set up to get big chunks of yardage at one time. The methodical nature of our offense had to change to a hurry-up style, getting to the next play as fast as possible. We scored pretty quickly and were down 21-20 with the extra point to come. There was a discussion between our coaches and our offensive captains persuaded them to go for two, and the win. We didn't have much to lose because we weren't expected to win anyway and we had already played a game that we could be proud of.

I was hoping that the play call would be run behind Reggie because no one wanted to win more than he did. That was the call and we ran it in to go ahead 22-21. Our sideline went crazy! Jeremy, a small senior wide receiver ran up and down the sideline pretending to shoot revolvers with both hands at our fans. He quickly got corrected by Coach Clark which is one of the most memorable corrections of the year. The problem was, the game was not over—we scored quicker than we needed to and Central had time for one more drive.

Fortunately, their offense wasn't designed to throw downfield and get big chunks of yardage either. We knew we had to make a stand one more time and find a way to get out of there with a long awaited win over our rival—and many of my closest friends. My body was in throbbing pain from the beating I was taking. The gimmick game plan had worked up to this point and we had held their offense to less than half of their average yardage per game. It was an incredible feat, but could we stop them one more time? Coach Clark took yet another gamble and put Brent, our tall skinny quarterback at safety. Brent was an exceptional athlete but he wasn't used to playing defense. But he was smart enough to do the one task he was told to do—knock the ball to the ground if it is thrown deep.

Their drive fell short after a couple of batted down passes and the game was over. I triumphantly fell to the ground in exhaustion and it took several minutes for me to join the celebration. I had never been so tired and drained, but I had never been so overjoyed either. We had pulled off the unthinkable. We had defeated Central for the first time in five long years and we had nudged our way into the playoff hunt. We would have to wait and see if Hueytown could pull off an upset against Jess Lanier and get some help in a couple of other games that were ongoing in order to extend our season. It didn't happen that way, and my high school football career was over. There are only two ways to end your career with a win; win a state championship, or win your final game of the regular season and miss the playoffs. As much as I would have loved to go on to the playoffs, I was thrilled that my last game as a Wildcat was a win against Central.

That night, just like most Friday nights, Reggie and I climbed in his truck and headed out to hang out with our friends. It was risky after this game, but we were all friends before, and we had hoped that hadn't changed. We had no intention of rubbing it in and we didn't feel like they would be sore about it and leave us out of our group. We were happy to find out that nothing had changed. We all sat around talking light-heartedly about the game and there was no animosity in our conversations. But I didn't see

Marty that night. That guy did a lot for me that night. He made me tougher and showed me that what some people see as dirty is just gamesmanship and he meant nothing by it. He and I still make social media jabs at each other from time to time, but its all in good fun. He was my biggest opponent ever and one on one, he probably got the best of me that night, but 22-21 was the score and we were on the better end of that.

I ended up getting several awards at the banquet that year but the one that I wanted over any other was Team Captain. There are Most Valuable Player Awards, All State awards, and All Star awards, but I wanted that Captain's plaque. I won the dedication award and received a plaque for being named to the All West Alabama Team by the Tuscaloosa Newspaper. The last award given was the Team Captain award and Coach Moore smiled as he called my name. I was more than honored. I walked up to the front of the decorated lunchroom in my ugly green sweater vest and got the award that I coveted since I watched Big Dusty get it in 1991. Being the captain of a team with almost a hundred players is an honor, and one that I worked hard for and was proud of.

In all of my successes of that season, I never gave a thought to God or Jesus being the reason I was able to do these things. My self-reliance became even stronger and I began to place football above everything; it was my god. I actually made the statement after that banquet when told that God had blessed me with great talent and work ethic that, "If God blessed me with all of that, I wouldn't have to work as hard as I do to be good at it." I really thought that God's blessings should come without the need to work for anything and everything I had achieved was because of me and the effort that I put into it. I wish I wasn't so blind back then. I wish that I had played for His glory alone—I would've had that platform that Coach Clark talked about. I took it all for granted and used it in the wrong way and removal happened again.

Chapter Fourteen

Booze and the Snooze Button

After the season was over, I kept working out as much as I could and took several trips to college campuses for visits with coaches that were recruiting me. Every place I visited had coaches talking on and on about grades and doing well in the classroom. I never really excelled in the classroom because I was under the impression that it wasn't that important. Yes, I had heard it all from college coaches about the importance of good grades but I thought it was just a lie. I took the minimal amount of classes that I needed to graduate and gave minimal efforts in those classes and did just enough to pass them. Graduating would be all that I needed to do in order to play in college; or so I thought.

I would sit in meetings with coaches and it began to be meetings about reasons why they can't give me a scholarship. Most of it had to do with my size and the positions that I played. Most linebackers in college were six inches taller than I was and weighed twenty pounds more and I wasn't even in the same atmosphere when it came to the size of the common college defensive lineman. A couple of coaches did say that they would take a chance on me and move me back to the offensive side of the ball as a fullback. The fullback was a dying position and most teams had gone away from utilizing one by replacing it with another receiver. So my options were shrinking. It motivated me to stay in the weight room and work even harder, but there was little that I could do about my height and weight.

My sister, Jackie had been at Troy State University for a couple of years so I was familiar with the surroundings and my cousin, Angela was planning to attend there as well. Troy State was one of those schools that still utilized a fullback in their "rabbit" offense. Their fullbacks were usually smaller than the typical fullbacks and caught passes more than usual. It was the perfect fit for me. The problem was they weren't one of the schools that paid me much attention. As my options started to get even smaller, I was called to the counselor's office. As with most of my meetings in the coach's office, I was clueless as to why I had been summoned to a place that I had never been before.

It was explained to me that the NCAA, the governing body of college athletics, had a new qualification formula known as the NCAA Clearinghouse. I had never heard of this and it was the first year that it was instituted and put into practice. I had qualifying test scores, was on track to graduate and had a grade point average that would allow me at least conditional entry into the colleges that I was considering. But to the NCAA, that wasn't enough. I was told that no matter what, I was one math credit and one science lab credit short of qualifying to play at an NCAA school for my first year. This was what was known as "Prop 48" and it meant that I would lose a year of eligibility. Prop 48 was for players that didn't have qualifying test scores or a high enough grade point average in the past, but now it was for people like me—those who did just enough in the classroom to get by and graduate.

Now, after being told all the reasons why some schools wouldn't give me a scholarship, they wouldn't have been allowed to anyway and I would have to walk on and sit out my first year. That would be a tough deal because at the time, Prop 48 walk on players didn't have access to the same things that scholarship players did. I wouldn't have coaches looking out for me, monitoring my grades, making sure I went to class and I wouldn't have the free study halls and tutoring either. I wouldn't be allowed to workout with the team, practice with the team or do anything else that college athletes get to do. I would have to workout at the school's recreation center, on my own and I would have to stay self-motivated to pull this off.

The only place that I was willing to do all of this at was Troy State University. I called Coach Turk who was in charge of the walk-ons and informed him that I would be coming there and I would be ready to play after my ineligibility year. I felt like I had achieved all that I had by doing it myself and I didn't need anyone to motivate me to get it done. I had Jackie and Angela there too so it wouldn't be like a foreign place to me. And one day, I would get to play for the legend, Coach Blakeney! The summer of 1994, as the date came for scholarship players to report to school, I was still in Northport waiting and it began to upset me. I couldn't figure out why I was being punished for a new qualifying formula that I wasn't aware of.

I started blaming everyone but myself. I blamed the counselor, my coaches and even blamed God. I was so angry that the feelings of self-reliance grew even stronger and my need for God was placed even further in the back of my mind. If I was blessed by God with talent and effort, why was He taking it all away from me for an entire year? It would be a year wasted and a year of struggle and all because of a new formula that was foreign to me. To be fair, my high school team mates that went on to play in college weren't aware of this new rule either, but they had done more than just get by in the classroom so it didn't effect them the way that it effected me. After all of MY hard work, after all of MY success and after all of MY efforts, it was all put on hold and it was God's fault—or at least someone's other than my own.

Hindsight Joy

I went on to Troy and moved into Alumni Hall and was ready for my year of hard work and preparation to make this all right—in my own power. When I got there, I made sure I knew where I could go and workout and where I could go and do some work on the field after I found someone that could help me that didn't play on the team. In the beginning, I did everything that I set out to do. I worked out every day and caught passes from a former high school quarterback that had no intentions to play in college because it would have gotten in the way of him getting a degree. One morning, I was on the intermural fields with him catching passes and one pass sailed a little high. I jumped up to catch it and when I came to the ground, I landed on my right shoulder. Of course I didn't have any pads on so it wasn't quite a soft landing. I felt a pop or a rip; something that didn't feel right and immediately it started to hurt.

At that point, there wasn't much that I could do about it because I didn't have the privilege of using athletic trainers or team doctors. The pain wasn't unbearable over the next few days, but it was impossible to lift weights and I couldn't get my arm up enough to catch any passes. So, suddenly, I had nothing to do except for attend the classes that I cared very little about. Again, anger started to creep into my heart again and I started to scream at God. I had not suffered an injury in football since the ninth grade. I had put my body through near torture in practice and in games and never had an injury that debilitated my abilities to work hard. And now I can't do anything because I had been hurt just catching a ball. Why was God taking away my ability to train and prepare for the next season? Why has He done this for the second time in just a few short months?

I didn't tell anyone about my injury because I just thought that it would heal itself. I was in good shape and I had always heard that a well conditioned body is the best way to heal an injury and even prevent them from happening. I didn't need a doctor or a trainer; I was okay with healing in my own. I began to miss a lot of classes. I didn't see much need for them when I was able to train and now I didn't have my training to motivate me to get out of the bed. My shoulder started to hurt worse and my anger towards God grew by the day. This was my first struggle with alcohol and depression.

In Troy, there was a gas station that would sell alcohol and cigarettes to a baby in diapers if no one else was in the store. It was easy to get anything that I wanted. My room mate was from a nearby town and always went home on the weekends and stayed with his high school friends on most nights. I rarely left my dorm room for the next few months as my shoulder got worse and my sadness turned to addiction. I would get a ride to this gas station and buy the cheapest wine that I could get and one pack of powdered Kool aid to pour into the bottle. I would then sit in my dorm all alone and drink until I went to sleep. This went from happening on the weekend to happening almost every night. My parents sent me $40 a week for spending money and that went a long way when my alcohol of choice only cost $1.79 per bottle. In my second quarter of school, I may have attended classes six times total.

My life had turned into a wreck and I masked it all with cheap alcohol and seclusion. Getting out and living the college life wasn't appealing to me without playing football and now it looked increasingly obvious that I would never play again. I couldn't find any worth to anything in my life anymore. One morning in April of 1995, I went to the recreation center and was going to try and lift weights. I hadn't even been in the weight room since September but I knew I had to do something. I would give it one last shot to see if I could regain what I used to be and maybe play again. It didn't take long for me to realize that I couldn't even lift a quarter of what I used to lift and the pain in my shoulder was worse than ever. It was over. I would never play again and it wasn't my fault! I spent the rest of that quarter in school hitting the snooze button and drinking myself to sleep, alone in my dorm room.

Soon I would have to go home to Northport and wait around until my grade report showed up in the mail and figure out a plan to keep Pop from killing me and momma from being disappointed in me. The embarrassment to come was troubling and I knew I would not be going back to Troy.

Chapter Fifteen

Second Chances and a Gallon of Water

For about a week after coming home from school, I struggled with what to do when my parents learned that I would not be going back. Many ideas came to my mind but nothing seemed to be a perfect idea. I started to think that I could tell them about how badly my shoulder was hurting but I knew that wouldn't be a reason not to at least return to school, and at the time, the pain in my shoulder was gone. Although my injury had healed, it was still too late to go back and try to get ready to play. I had already failed every class that I was enrolled in but one and I had stopped communicating with Coach Turk. My playing days were over.

When my grade report came in the mail, I still had not devised a plan of action. My mom got the mail that day and she was very upset but she wasn't giving up on me doing something with my life. She mentioned that I should take the Armed Forces exam and go into the Air Force. I was a Broadcast Journalism major at Troy and I was hoping to be a TV weatherman and meteorologist. What I ended up doing with my life is not even in the same atmosphere as that. But I found out that the Air Force was a good avenue to take to get into meteorology and the Air Force actually had pilots that flew into storms. That was it! Not only was it a good plan to keep Pop from dismantling me limb by limb, but it was a good plan that excited me and I could still enter the career that I wanted to be in—and the Air Force would pay for me to go back to college when I was done.

Pop was all for that plan and I had dodged a bullet! He was pretty mad at me for my lack of fortitude in dealing with adversity in Troy. But he encouraged me in my new plan of action and I immediately signed up to take the test. I met with a recruiter and set it all up. I took the exam on a Saturday and I felt like I was taking a college entrance exam. I scored as high as a person could score and the recruiter showed me all of the career options that I could enter through the Air Force and meteorology was one of them! I was fired up and couldn't wait to get started. We set up a day and time for my entrance physical which was about three weeks away.

For the next three weeks I spent most of my time running around seeing all of my old friends that were still in town and having as much fun as I could before entering a time that I knew wouldn't be much fun. I was still struggling with alcohol at the time and I drank almost every night. One night, a few of us were on the straightaway in front of the school when a police officer pulled up. A friend of mine from Troy had come to spend the weekend with me. We had a cooler full of beer and a bottle of cheap whiskey in his car with us. The officer saw it all by just peeking into the window. I just knew my date to ship out to Basic Training was going to be changed or maybe I wouldn't even be able to go at all. Fortunately, the officer was lenient and gave each of us a sobriety test and let the only sober one, Anthony, my friend from Troy, drive us all home—but not before he made us pour out all of our beverages.

I had dodged another bullet! All I could think of was how I would explain to my parents that I had wasted away another opportunity to be something in life. I learned really quickly that I had better walk a straight and narrow line until I left for Basic Training or that would all be gone too. I was really beginning to doubt that I would ever get to my departure date because everything that was happening. In less than one year, I went from training to play football in college to a college dropout and on the verge of going to jail a time or two for stupid decisions. I decided that I would find a way to make it all happen. I reminded myself that I accomplished a lot in the past, on my own, with no help from anyone. I was confident in myself, and I didn't seek any guidance or direction from any other person or place. I was now my own god. I didn't have football anymore, but now I had myself, and I thought that was enough. This would have been a great time to have Jesus in my life for strength.

I had dodged enough trouble and my departure date had finally arrived. I caught a van from the recruiter's office to Montgomery where we would have the military style physical on the next morning and after passing that, we would leave for San Antonio's Lackland Air Force Base for Basic Training. When we got to Montgomery, they put us in a hotel that used to be a train station. It was a pretty cool place and I just spent that night sitting in my hotel room revisiting things in my past. I remembered in agony all of the opportunities that I messed up and couldn't stop thinking about how life would have been if I had just been wiser. But arrogance was still an issue in my life and I just knew that I would get through this next chapter in my life with no problems; I just needed to get on that flight to San Antonio.

The physical was bright and early the next morning. A shuttle bus picked us up and took us to the clinic where we would spend the next few hours being tested for any physical ailments that could keep us from enlisting. At the time I was around one hundred-ninety pounds and still in good physical condition. But that weight at my height was considered obese according to military requirements. They told me before I went to Montgomery that there was a different method for people considered overweight due to build and body make up, but in good condition. They would measure my waist, just at the belly button, and then measure my neck and subtract and use that formula to gauge whether my weight was high because of being out of shape or because that's just how I was built. There shouldn't be any issue with that, or at least I thought.

When my group was called in, the first stop was to be drug screened by urine sample. I had gone to the restroom just after breakfast and I shouldn't have. I couldn't produce a sample. Because I couldn't get the job done, they made me drink a gallon of water and fall back in line at the NEXT station. The drug screen would now have to be the very last stop. Of course I begged to go back and give a urine sample because I was now full of water and my stomach was about to explode. A gallon of water will do a lot to expand your belly. After going through a couple of stops, we came to the height and weight station. I already knew I would be overweight so I would be measured. They moved me on into another room where they took out a tape measurer and ran it around my expanded belly. Obviously, because of the water I had just drank, I failed that part. I asked if I could go give the sample and come back and they said I couldn't and I had failed the physical.

I was sent back out to the lobby where I would have to wait three more hours for the shuttle to come back and take us to the hotel. The officer in the lobby told me that I could not go to sleep, but I did anyway. I wasn't going to let them tell ME what to do—I failed the physical and I was no longer under their authority. I could have stayed awake, but in my defiant ways, I rebelled just to see what would happen. I got yelled at by a Marine recruiter and of course I snapped back at him and that exchange sealed my fate in terms of being able to come back for the next departure date. That didn't bother me though, I was confident in myself that another plan would come along and I would be fine; by myself!

The ride home was long and painful. I had to come up with what I would tell my parents about why I blew another chance to be something. I wasn't able to come up with anything. I was clueless. I didn't want to go back to school even if it was at the local community college. I didn't want to get a job either. On the way home, my shoulder started to really hurt. It hadn't been a problem for a while and this pain was unexplainable. I didn't remember doing anything to it that would have reinjured it. I went through all the exercises with the Air Force recruits and had no problems with it. I again just shrugged it off thinking that it would go away.

When I got back home, I had a long talk with my parents and the conclusion was that I had to go find a job. I agreed, but I wanted to do more with my life than just an entry level job. But Pop wasn't willing to let me lie around and do nothing while I devise a plan of action, so I got a job as a maintenance assistant at a local apartment complex. The pay was terrible but I made enough to go buy my first car. Now with a car payment and insurance to pay, there was no way I could go back to school. I enjoyed my job, a little bit anyway, but it just wasn't something that I could be proud of. It wasn't a career that I could feel good about; it was just another part of peoples' conversation when they talked about how much I had messed up in the last year. I had to change something and it needed to be quick. My pride was just too damaged to stay on the same path.

I never could stop thinking about playing football and different ideas about how I could make that happen crossed my mind hundreds of times a day. One afternoon, I found the business card of Coach Spillman, the coach from the Junior College in Mississippi that I had met at the Cowboy's camp. I called the number on the card and was told that Coach Spillman was no longer coaching there. I told the man that answered the phone what my name was at the beginning of the call and I guess he wrote it down because the very next day he called me back. He said that he found notes on me that the previous staff had made and filed away. He then invited me to a fully padded, full contact tryout a couple of weeks later.

Here it was! This was my chance to go back and play football. I hurried to the field house at County High and talked to Coach Moore about it. All he said was, "Let's go to the equipment room and suit you up. You'll probably have to bring your own equipment." His simple reaction was all I needed to know that I needed to go do this. I worked hard leading up to that day so I could get back in shape and maybe sweat out some of the substances that I had been consuming for over a year. The time had come and I was ready to get my life back on track, on my own, with no help from anyone! I was back to placing my hope on football.

Chapter Sixteen

Back in the Game...But How?

Back in February of 1996, a terrible ice storm crippled the Tuscaloosa area and most people were homebound for several days. I had traded in my first car on a little four-wheel-drive truck so I could decrease my payments and maybe find a way to go back to school one day. The ice storm didn't stop me and my friends from getting around. A lifelong friend of mine and team mate, Casey, had an apartment on the river and I would drive around in my truck and pick people up to come to his apartment to hang out. One evening as I arrived with a small load of friends, I walked in the dining room and saw a girl that I didn't know. She had a dark complexion and dark hair. I thought she was Puerto Rican and I instantly knew that I had to talk to her, but I locked up with fear and the whole night went by without a single word and then she was gone.

I couldn't sleep that night from thinking about the opportunity that I let pass me by. The next morning, I asked around about who she was and all that I could get from anyone was who her older sister was. Farrah was a year younger than us and I knew who she was but had no clue that she had a sister. That night as the ice began to melt away and people started showing back up at Casey's apartment, I was told that Erica wanted to meet me. I didn't even know who Erica was until I asked if she was that Puerto Rican-looking girl. It was her and she was coming back that night. We finally had a few small conversations that night and I offered to drive her home when her curfew came.

We began dating soon after and were still together that summer when it came time for me to go try out in Mississippi. We had a lot of fun together for the months leading up to the tryout. I had moved out of my parents' house and rented a small house in the center of Northport with Brian, a guy that I was working with at the time. Of course this was all before I learned of the tryout. When the tryout was scheduled, I had to tell Brian that if I made the team, I would be leaving. The longer I was around Erica, more thoughts of passing on the football tryout came across my mind, but I was going to go through with it anyway and just see what would happen.

Momma went with me to Mississippi that Saturday. I was pretty nervous because I hadn't had any full contact in quite some time. Momma said it was like riding a bike—when it starts, I'll pick right up where I left off because you never forget how to play. She was right. We started off stretching and I realized that flexibility was a thing of the past for me. I was worried that I would end up tearing a muscle out there and have one more issue to go along with my shoulder which was still bothering me. When we split up into positions, the coaches sent me with the fullbacks and running backs. I guess the old staff had me penciled in as a fullback just like everyone else that recruited me. I decided right then that I would attack these drills with a linebacker's mentality and be a violent as I could be.

The first drill had us run to a point and turn up the field inside two cones where a defender would try to tackle us. We were told to 'make a move and make them miss'. I refused to dance around anyone! I didn't do as I was told. I would use the momentum that I had from running to that point and lower my head and run right over the defender in an effort to catch some attention and maybe even destroy the other guy's desire to be between those cones. I didn't get tackled one single time. It reminded me of that time at the Cowboy's camp during the camp-ending game when we were supposed to grab a flag but I insisted on tackling. I was all about doing what I wanted to do and not what someone told me to do.

The tryout went that way for the entire day. I lowered my head every chance I had and refused to dance. The coaches attempted to correct me a few times but it didn't work. I kept destroying defenders and kept everyone looking at me. A friend of mine, Jake, who played summer league baseball with me, was already at the college as a quarterback. He and his team mates came out to watch and I was the talk of the team. After the tryout was over, a few guys were called over to talk to the head coach—I was not one of them. I figured they didn't like the fact that I defied their orders all day and I wouldn't be asked to join the team. The coach that invited me walked up and complimented me on my aggressiveness and intensity and said he would be in touch. But why wasn't I called over to the head coach in that group?

The ride home was brutal and full of questions. Did my insubordination outweigh my ability to lay the hammer on everyone that tried to stop me? Would that defiance cost me another chance to play football? It was terrible waiting for that call over the next week. After a few days I just thought that by the coach telling me that he would be in touch, he was actually saying "Get off our campus, you can't play here". I actually waited by the phone for hours a day hoping to get a call. It finally happened. The coach was on the other end and asked how I was doing. I told him that other than the huge bruise across my forehead that changed colors overnight, every night, I was feeling pretty good—but in reality, my shoulder was throbbing in pain.

He asked how interested I was in coming to play there and I replied that it was all I had been thinking about since I left. I was offered a chance to come join the team, but they were out of scholarship money at the time but there was a chance that a scholarship player wouldn't show up to camp and I would be the next in line. Their school was very inexpensive to attend so I decided that I would take the opportunity. I finally told momma and Pop about my shoulder and that I would need to get it checked out before I left that summer. It was late spring at the time that I went to the doctor. I really wasn't concerned about the pending diagnosis, there was no way it was going to stop me from playing. If I needed some physical therapy, I had plenty of time to get it done before I left in August.

After the first visit, they scheduled me for an MRI because my shoulder was making some unusual noises and they couldn't see a lot from a simple X-ray. That was my first experience with an MRI machine and it was awful. I've never been really good being in tight spaces, especially when there are loud noises going on all around me. It was something I never wanted to do again! The results came back and it was bad. My 'glenoid labrum' was completely torn and the cartilage in my shoulder was almost gone. The doctor said he would need to go in there with a scope and hope that the repairs would be minimal, but he wouldn't know until he got in there to see. The troubling thing was when he told me that I wouldn't know how bad it was until I woke up from the surgery.

I still wasn't too worried. I had a minor surgery on my right elbow in the past and I was back training in no time. I didn't see that this would be any different. Jackie was graduating from Troy State that weekend and my surgery was on Friday. I figured that I would have the surgery and go home the same day and be able to go down for her graduation. It didn't quite happen that way, though. When I woke up in the recovery room, I was informed that it was even worse than it looked at the beginning and the doctor had to completely repair my shoulder, cartilage and ligaments. It was obvious to the surgeon that this was an old injury that had worsened over time because I ignored it. I was in the hospital for several days for pain management and missed my sister's graduation. That was hurtful enough, but then I realized that I likely wouldn't be ready for football camp in August.

When I was alert enough to ask the questions, I did; 'will I be ready for practice in August?' Worst case scenario, I thought, would be that I would miss the upcoming season and be able to come back the next summer. That didn't seem to be too awful because by then, the school would have more money to put toward my tuition. The answer I got was far beyond what I thought to be the worst case. Not only would I not be ready for the upcoming season, I would not be able to play football at all, forever. There was too much permanent damage done that likely wouldn't hold up to the contact that I would be involved in during a college football season.

There I was again, wondering why nothing ever went as planned. I had made plenty of dumb decisions in the past that had cost me opportunities, but I was even more angry this time because this time, it wasn't my fault. Again I blamed God. Football was my passion and it consumed my life. It was my god again and it was removed from my life again. I realized that everything that I placed the utmost faith in was always removed from my life either due to my poor choices or something that I couldn't do anything about. The reality of the situation was, if I had done more than just get by in high school, I wouldn't have missed that first season at Troy and I wouldn't have gotten hurt in the first place. And if I had gotten hurt anyway, I would have had trainers taking care of the injury and it wouldn't have been nearly as damaging in the long run.

The whole list of life events that led me to that hospital bed continued to run through my head and I grew even angrier. I was so conceited with myself that I placed none of the blame on me and all on God and anyone else that I could use to pass it off on. I wouldn't even be able to go back to my job because it required a lot of use from my right arm which would be unusable for a long time. It just kept getting worse. Momma came to the hospital after she got back from graduation and by that time, my anger was at its worst. Of course she always had a 'bright side' to everything. She suggested that I become a coach. At the time I wasn't even thinking about that and shrugged it off as a terrible idea.

Her suggestion began to sit on me and I was warming up to it. I knew of a lot of great players that were awful coaches and I didn't want to be a bad coach if it was something that I wanted to do. At that time, I was working for Coach Jimmy Burns, one of my little league coaches from years earlier. I called him when I got out of the hospital and asked if they needed any assistant coaches for the upcoming season. He was still really involved in the league and was the President of the Northport association. He told me that they didn't need any assistants but he wanted me to be the head coach of the nine and ten-year-old team. After mulling it over for a few days, I accepted. When practice was to start, I knew I would still be in the middle of rehabilitating my shoulder after surgery and I would still have my arm bound to my side. My journey to being a football coach had begun.

Chapter Seventeen

Ready or Not, Here Comes Buck

After I got out of the hospital, I went to stay with Nana for a little while. She was retired and would help me with the everyday things that I couldn't do with one arm. She also had satellite television which wasn't very common at the time. We both loved watching the Atlanta Braves and whatever kind of wrestling that we could find. On that particular satellite service, it wasn't hard to find a wrestling show, especially late at night. I spent a lot of my time in her new leather recliner watching TV especially after she went to bed. She would make supper during the Braves game and after we ate and the game was over, she would go to bed and I would flip through the hundreds of channels until I found some scripted violence. Before she went to bed, she would always give me my medicine and make sure I had everything I needed.

My bedtime dose of pain medicine was larger than the ones I took throughout the day. I was given more so I could sleep as pain free as I could. But I never went right to bed because of all of those channels. I started to really enjoy sitting there with the high that I got from the double dose of narcotics. This was when I first developed an addiction to pain killers. It wasn't an abuse just yet since they were prescribed and I was taking them as directed, but I was hooked nonetheless. It never crossed my mind that this would become a problem for me later on; I was just enjoying it while I could.

As I got a little bit better, I was able to drive and go see Erica a couple nights a week. She was still in high school so I was always home early. One night while I was at her house, she expressed a concern that she might be pregnant. She tried to explain to me the reasons that she felt that way, but I didn't understand any of it and kind of ignored the possibility. I knew it wouldn't happen because I was out of work and she was so young and I wasn't ready to be a father. I just didn't think that God would allow me to have a child since I was so irresponsible with everything else in my life at the time. He had been taking everything I loved out of my life so why would He insert something so important like a child into it at a time when I was so helpless and Erica still had a year left in school?

She told me as I left that night that she would be taking a home pregnancy test after I left and she would let me know the results. The drive home was another one of those nervous times where so many things went through my head that it began to hurt. I just couldn't wait to get home and take my double dose of medicine and forget all about the test results. When I called her to let her know I had got to Nana's, she told me that test was positive, meaning she was pretty certain that we would be expecting a child. Her mother, Valerie would be taking her to the doctor the next day to get confirmation and I just put the thought to the back of mind and grabbed the remote to the television and went about my opioid induced evening. I vividly remember our conversation that night as I stood in the hallway of Nana's house discussing what we were going to do. There was never a question of whether or not we would go through with this pregnancy, the question was, how would I support a child and get her all the things that she needed while I couldn't work.

The doctor's appointment confirmed what the home test concluded. I had to face her parents, who were active believers and followers of Jesus. They were upset, but supportive and felt like somehow, this child would be a certain blessing to all of us. The next step was telling my parents that I had again diverted from the path that I had set for my life. After a two-year span where everything was being taken from me, God was giving me something of utmost importance, a child, but I wasn't asking for it. We talked to my parents one evening when Erica came over for supper. I'm not quite sure how we broke the news to them, but I do recall my mom just getting up and walking out of the room. Pop just sat there in his usual pose—his right leg under his left leg, in his chair and a glass of sweet tea sweating in his hand. He brought up the fact that since I already called him Pop, he wouldn't have to come up with some catchy name as a grandfather.

Mom eventually came back in the room after spending some time in silence in her bedroom. In her unconditional, loving way, she gave us her support that she would do whatever she could to make this work. The pressure of telling your parents that you were bringing a child into this world is intense. Over the last two years, I had those feelings a time or two when having to break some bad news to them, but this time it was worse. I was barely twenty years old and Erica had not even started her senior year in high school and we were about to have the biggest responsibility that a person could ever have. The two families met together one evening and it was obvious that we had a lot of love and support even though we had made such a mistake. Later on, we would understand how important this child would be to everyone that loves him.

Erica and I decided that we would get married some time after the baby was born. He was due to enter the world in early March. I coached the nine and ten-year-old team that fall as we awaited the baby's arrival. My shoulder was healing and I was again searching for work. I would end up moving from job to job quite frequently over the next few years. I just never could find my place in the job market and never was happy doing anything. I just knew that one day I would make a living coaching football, I just didn't know how that would happen since it would be nearly impossible to father a child and go back to school. Momma kept insisting that I could do it.

I went to work as a security guard at the hospital in Tuscaloosa. I was on the dreaded midnight shift and usually had the honor of patrolling the emergency department parking lot. On weekends, that parking lot stayed busy and dramatic. On any given night, family and loved ones of patients would come through that lot and some were there for other reasons. One night after midnight, there was a shooting on the west side of town and the victim was brought by ambulance to the hospital. I was alerted that the shooter could be coming to the hospital to 'finish off' his rival. I was given his description and told to be on the lookout for his car.

After convincing myself numerous times that the shooter wouldn't come there, I just forgot about it and kept walking around the lot. After a good while, my guard came down and a car came speeding into the parking lot. As I hurried into a spot where I could see what kind of car it was, I realized that it was the shooter's car, or at least one that fit its description. The city police officer that was placed there in case the shooter came looking for his enemy was inside using the restroom and I was all alone out in that lot with the shooter. I walked as fast as I could to a spot that could interrupt his entrance into the hospital. When he approached me, he wasted no time pulling out his weapon and aiming it right at my face. I knew I couldn't back down because the guards at the entrance doors were older gentlemen and I though very highly of my toughness even when looking down the barrel of a pistol.

I couldn't believe I was in this situation, especially since this job didn't pay me anywhere close to a wage that would be worth losing my life over. Erica was getting close to her due date and I knew I shouldn't be risking my life to keep something from happening to other people that I didn't even know. But I stood my ground and the incident ended without anything happening. There was no plaque of appreciation, no medal of honor and no ceremony for me, just a new work schedule for the following week. One night before I went in to work, I stopped by to see Erica. She was due any time but I didn't think it would be that night.

I went home to get dressed for work but before I left the house, Valerie called and said it was time to go to the hospital. I was in no shape to drive to the hospital so Reggie came to drive me. I was a bundle of nerves on that drive too. Its amazing how many times that I have had extremely nervous times on a drive in a car. I called my supervisor to inform them that I would be at the hospital but would not be reporting to work because my son was about to be born. There were no congratulations, instead I was told to come by the headquarters and sign a form stating that I was consenting to the punishment I would get for calling in so close to the start of my shift. When I refused to come sign the document, I was fired—on the night my child was born.

Losing my job that night was quickly forgotten. It was really a good thing because I would no longer have to risk my life for pennies and I was not going to miss the birth of my child. We didn't have to wait very long after Erica arrived at the hospital. Logan Carl Brehm—or Buck as I have always called him--was born in the early morning hours of March 5, 1997. I still remember being able to carry him down the hall to the nursery. It was a feeling that I could have never imagined. I knew I had a little future star. I couldn't sleep for a few days because I would sit at the hospital and stay at the window where they had my son sleeping. I couldn't get enough of just looking at him. Erica had a few minor issues in the hospital with pain, but she healed quickly and we were able to take them home.

For the first couple of months, I could just visit them because they were living with Erica's parents. I had started a job in a lumber warehouse and was trying to save enough money to get an apartment so they could come live with me after Erica graduated from high school. In May, I was able to get a small one-bedroom apartment in Northport and at the beginning of June, Erica and Logan were able to move in with me and we started our little family. I again changed jobs and went to work for a construction company and I worked a lot of hours on the road. I didn't like getting home late and leaving Erica at home to care for Logan. It wasn't the ideal situation starting off, but it was all that I could do.

When Logan got to an age that we were comfortable with him going to day care, Erica got a job as a day care worker. It was perfect because she could work and Logan could be there with her; and tuition was free. After long days at work, I would usually come home with a 12-pack of beer and would wait for them to go to sleep and drink until I eventually fell asleep. It wasn't an every night thing, but it was an every Monday night thing. It was wrestling night and the two biggest wrestling companies in the world were in the prime of their Monday Night Wars. It was three solid hours of wrestling and it just gave me an excuse to drink far more than I should have.

Our marriage didn't really get off to a great start. We had money issues from the beginning and it was really not of her doing. She was trying to be a mother and work as much as possible and I worked a lot of hours and never had a lot to show for it. Bills were always behind and there were a lot of times where some kind of utility was turned off due to nonpayment. Money issues caused a lot of fights and we had to move around at the end of each lease that we had. We did have some good times though. There were stretches of time where the bills were getting paid and money wasn't an issue. But I was still bouncing from job to job and it was just not something that I had planned for my life and it started to bother me.

I tried everything to get in to a career that made a difference. I went to work at an Alabama State Prison as a Corrections Cadet as I awaited my turn to attend the Corrections Academy in Selma. I really enjoyed that job and it looked as if I would be in corrections or law enforcement for the rest of my working life. IT was an honorable job and I was proud to tell people what I did for a living. After working at the prison for twelve weeks, I reported for the academy and I felt like it would be an easy thing for me. In the pre-academy testing, I was first in all of the physical fitness tests except the long run. I have had a problem with long distance running because of my shins, but I wasn't going to let that keep me from graduating.

The Academy started off great. I was doing well in the classroom and had the best scores in the fitness tests again. On the sixth day, we would go out for that long run again. In this academy, if you fail to do any of the required tasks, you fail and have to leave. In our case, we would also lose our job. My roommate and I did all that knew to do to prepare my shins for this run. I started at a great pace in the middle of the pack. At the halfway point I was easily on pace to finish in under the required time, by a large margin. My shins were holding up just fine; until I got about three-quarters of the way down the last stretch of the run. I was within a quarter of a mile from the finish when it happened.

My right shin had tightened up so badly that it began to spasm and I went straight to the ground. I tried to get up and then my left shin did the same. I still battled to my feet until the pain became so bad that I could no longer move my foot at the ankle joint. I was done and couldn't get off the road. A State Trooper car picked me up and carried me to the dorm building where I was told to pack my things and leave. I had lost yet another job and this time I was devastated. There was nothing else that I could do to have a respectable career. I wanted to supply every need that my wife and Logan had and now I didn't know how I would accomplish that. All of my gifts and talents appeared to be physical and this felt like my last chance to be something respectable. But, momma still only had one idea, and she repeated this idea again and again. She knew that at some point I would eventually listen to her and give it a try.

Chapter Eighteen

Have You Seen the Newspaper Today?

After I got home from the Academy, five weeks earlier than anyone expected, I explained to Erica what happened. She was pretty upset about it, but by this time, it was somewhat common for me to be looking for work. I went back to doing construction just to make sure that we didn't get too far behind on bills and Logan would have food. Erica's grandmother Hazel adored Logan. We would always go sit with her husband who was bedridden every Saturday while she got out of the house, usually to get her hair done. Every Saturday when we got to her house, she always had plenty of baby formula, food and diapers for Logan. She made life as young parents a lot easier for us. But it just wasn't enough and as much as I appreciated the help, I wanted to do it on my own.

I would call momma on occasion and just vent my frustrations about my career path or lack thereof. And every time, she would tell me the same thing, "You need to go back to school, I think God is calling you to be a football coach". I really didn't care what she thought God was calling me to do. I was still blaming Him for everything that had been happening to me

111

since I left Troy. But deep down, coaching is exactly what I wanted to do; I just didn't want the road that it would take to be able to do it as a career. I coached the little league team for two more years after Logan was born and I absolutely loved it. In three seasons we only lost two games. It looked like I had a small talent for motivating kids to play hard and I was gaining more knowledge of the game from the coaching end of it all.

One evening as my mom gave me the same line of advice, I decided to make a deal with her just to get her off my back for a while. Before I made this deal, we talked a lot about Coach Clark and how much he meant to me and how much I admired him as a man and a coach. Other than the obvious men in my life, Coach Clark was the most influential man in my life. He had moved on from County High and was the defensive coordinator somewhere in Georgia before he came back to Alabama. He had still not been selected as a head coach. I told mom that if Coach Clark gets a head coaching job, I will go back to school and get an education degree and make it my goal to coach on his staff. She was good with that deal and she actually left me alone about it—for a while anyway.

I had not even thought about that conversation for about a year until my phone rang one morning in spring of 1999. It was mom and I could tell she was excited about something. "Have you seen the newspaper today, son?" Of course I had not because I didn't subscribe to the local paper and the internet wasn't as informative as it is today. After asking her several times to tell me why she was asking me this, I finally just got off the phone and jumped in my truck and drove to the gas station up the street from our third home in three years. I put my fifty cents in the paper machine and pulled out the day's edition. I still wasn't really sure exactly where this information was inside the paper.

I scanned the local section, the national section, the weather section, the obituaries and the police report thinking someone we knew had been arrested. I didn't see anything that would've caused momma to call in excitement to see if I had read it. I left the Sports section for last, thinking that she rarely reads that section so it couldn't have come from there. There it was, in plain sight on the front of the Sports section. I knew without even reading the entire headline why momma was stoked and couldn't wait to call me. 'Former Tuscaloosa County Defensive Coordinator Named Head Football Coach at Prattville High'.

Coach Clark had finally got a head coaching job and this wasn't just a small job either. Prattville had previously had a dominant run in the early 1980's. In fact, on the first weekend in December of 1984 when we moved to Alabama, we went to watch them play in Legion Field in Birmingham for the state championship, which they won. In Alabama, if your school wins a championship, the supporters of the program expect you to win another one. Although it had been fifteen years since Prattville won a championship, the expectations were huge and Coach Clark had a big task on his hands. He didn't start small; he started at one of the largest schools in the state and one of the most successful in terms of winning percentage. But I knew he would be great there.

I also knew that I made a deal with momma, and she expected me to hold up my end of that deal. Erica and I had the discussion about me going to night school at a local community college to get the rest of my basic courses finished and I could still work during the day, but we would have to wait until Logan got a little bit older. I ran that plan by momma and she was fine with it but informed me that she would make sure that I followed through with my promise when that time came. The timing just wasn't quite right at the time in 1999.

Coach Clark's team won 7 games and lost 3 in his first year, a rather successful season for a first year coach at a high profile school. That would actually be his worst year throughout his nine-year career at the school. His final record after nine years as the head coach was 106 wins against only 11 losses. He won two state championships and won every region game for his last six seasons, 42 in a row. His last two teams were undefeated on the year. It is one of the most remarkable decade-long coaching stints in the history of

Alabama High School Football. I knew that he would be great before he started and he just proved why I admired him so much.

It wasn't so much about winning all of those games that made Coach Clark the man that I would try to be like; it was the way that he did it. He did everything with integrity and honor and did it all for God's glory. He never hid his faith from his players and even at a time when that didn't impress me much, I still remembered it. He got the best out of my undersized stature and I know that I wouldn't have been the player that I was without playing for him. I still had not seen or talked to him since he left for Georgia and at one point just prior to the day I went to get the newspaper, there was a rumor that he had been killed in a car accident. I spent a few days trying to get confirmation of the rumor and it took a while to finally learn that it wasn't true.

One summer I found out that he would be bringing his team to County High to play in a preseason jamboree game. I was excited about the chance to see him. Logan was five at the time and he and I went to the game with small hopes of being able to talk to him. We went early enough that there may be a chance to speak to him as they came out of the locker room for warm ups. When we walked in the gate, his team was sitting in the end zone bleachers and he was standing behind them. I rustled up the nerve to go speak to him thinking there was little chance that he would even remember me without me reminding him. Much to my surprise, he spotted me before I even got to him and he walked to meet me halfway.

He hugged me and said he was glad to see me and I quickly introduced him to my son. It was such an honor to have Logan meet the man that I admired more than any man in the world aside from Pop. Coach Clark bent down and shook Logan's hand and told him, "Your daddy is one of the best defensive linemen that I have ever coached, he was a terrific player and I bet you will be one too". No better compliment had ever been made about me, in my eyes anyway. I was almost brought to tears just that he remembered me and then having him say such great things about the player that I was. We talked for a little while about the past and the present and just before he took his team to the field, I told him I was going back to school in the spring so I could coach for him one day. As he shook my hand he said, "When you graduate, call me, and we will make that happen".

There was no question in my mind after that conversation that I was indeed going to go back to school. That very week, I visited the community college and took the steps to enroll for the next semester that was to start in January 2003. I was a little surprised at the support that I received from Erica about it, but she assured me that we would make it work as long as I did well in classes and worked during the day. It was the beginning of a difficult road to a degree.

Chapter Nineteen

Back to School

It had been over eight years since I sat in a classroom as a student. After a gap in education and working for the last several years, I knew it would be difficult to go to class since there would be no one making sure I attended. If you have a boss at a job, you are required to report to work, but now I was a twenty-five-year-old college Freshman with no boss and really no accountability to anyone but myself. I really didn't want to disappoint my momma; I had done enough of that in recent years. I really had motivation to do well because I had a young son that deserved to have a successful daddy and that's what I wanted to be for him. Further increasing my motivation was my desire to stop the money issues that were wrecking my marriage. Although the years that I would be in school would be tough financially, I knew that after it was all over with, I would be able to make a good living.

I was willing to do whatever I had to do to make ends meet while attending school at night. For the first year, I stretched myself and my time very thin. I took a job delivering newspapers early in the morning. After I had been doing that for about a month, another delivery route became available and instead of changing routes, I took the open one AND stayed on my original one. Delivering papers was sort of therapeutic for me. It was a tough job, but it was relaxing being on the road all alone in the early morning hours and creating challenges for myself in throwing papers to an exact spot without slowing down. Running two routes was difficult to pull off. I had to be at the warehouse two hours earlier and still get the deliveries done by a certain time, usually 6:00 a.m.

After finishing my routes each morning, I would come home and help get Logan ready for school. We had moved into a smaller apartment to save a little money on rent. Logan was in kindergarten at the time and wasn't ready to ride the bus yet, so I would drive him to school on most mornings. After dropping him off, I would go to work at a wine and beverage distribution company merchandising product. I would drive from store to store setting up displays and shelving all the stuff that the delivery truck dropped off each morning. That job was tough because I had time deadlines that I had to meet and store managers that I had to keep satisfied. A typical day on that job usually lasted until about 2:30 in the afternoon.

I would usually get home around 3:30 after picking Logan up from school and try to have supper done for Erica when she got home around 5:15. Then, I would hurriedly rush out the door to get to school by 6:00. Most days, my classes lasted until 8:30 p.m. and I would run home to sleep a couple of hours before getting up at 1:30 a.m. to repeat it all over again. It wasn't easy, but it was necessary. In the summer, I started thinking about coaching again. I couldn't go back to coaching little league because their practices were late in the evening and it would interfere with school. I was watching the news one evening and watched a story about a powder puff game that a local high school was having and saw that Joey Milligan was a coach for one of the teams. I emailed him at the school and asked if they had any room for a defensive coach on the varsity football staff. It was a long shot at the time, but they in fact had a spot for linebackers coach. After talking to Erica about it, I accepted the job as a volunteer and my high school coaching career had begun.

Now, I had to add football practice to that already hectic schedule and find a way to make that work. We knew that being a volunteer coach while in school was critical to build a resume worthy of hiring after graduation. In August of 2003, I started summer football practice as the linebackers coach of the brand new Paul W. Bryant High School Stampede. Bryant High was one of two schools that came out of the old Central High, our old football rivals. Our team had a lot of really talented athletes and my linebacker group was no exception. I had some really special players and my first coaching job was fairly simple; teach gifted athletes how to get to the football.

I was really enjoying this chapter in my life but the busy schedule was really starting to get to me and I quit running my paper routes. I still needed to find a way to make some of that money back, but there just wasn't enough time in the day. If I was going to find another part time job, it would have to be in the evening before bedtime. Our offensive coordinator, Darrin Hughes, was part of his family's parking lot maintenance company and they were looking for a sweeper truck operator cleaning parking lots at night. I rode with him one night and realized it was an easy job and I could actually manage to do this starting at 9:00 p.m. instead of 1:30 a.m. like I was doing delivering papers. On most nights, I would finish about 1:30 and have time to go home and sleep for a few hours.

My busy schedule continued through that first season at Bryant. We finished with a record of 3-7 but five of those losses were by less than a touchdown. We were close in every game and had a solid foundation to build the program from. We only had two seniors that season and I was getting all of my linebackers back for the next season. Things were going well in football and I was doing quite well in the classroom. Money was still a problem no matter how much I was trying to work and it was making home life pretty difficult.

Nana had passed away a few years earlier and her house had been empty for a while. It was a small house at the bottom of the hill from

Momma and Pop's house. We moved in the little house so we wouldn't have to pay rent and the utilities were very affordable, even for us. I had finished my classes at the community college and transferred to the University of West Alabama which was about a fifty-minute drive from the house. At the time, gasoline prices were higher than they had ever been at over four dollars per gallon. The money that we were saving from rent and low utilities was being dumped in my gas tank just so I could get to school every day. Even with Erica and I being as frugal as we could with what little money we had, it was still a problem.

There were times that Erica and I would go days without speaking—even if we were both home. I slept on the couch every night and I would be gone before she and Logan got out of bed. It was a bad time in our marriage and it was due in large part to money and bills that just weren't getting paid. It was obvious that we really didn't love each other and didn't really care much about our marriage. The only times we actually spoke was on nights that Logan was with my parents and we went out on the town with friends. But then Monday would come, and the strain on our marriage would intensify. As I look back on our troubles, its obvious that money was the problem, but the lack of our faith in Christ was the root of it all.

In the whole time that we were married—eight years total—we may have attended a regular church service three times and mostly on Easter when it followed a Saturday night of heavy drinking and bar hopping. We never talked about Jesus with Logan and never took him to church. Logan wasn't lacking in his faith in Christ though, thanks to my parents and Erica's. We both had faithful parents and they took the time to show Logan the love of Jesus and the beauty of the gospel. I am so grateful that they all took the time and the effort to do this while Erica and I stayed focused on worldly things such as money. As Logan grew up, he loved attending church and being with his grandparents because they were the only ones that actually took him there. In hindsight, it is saddening to me that I wasn't the man who introduced his son to Jesus, but the important thing is, he knows Him and He still follows Him.

Royce C. Brehm

Chapter Twenty

The Collapse of a Godless Marriage

We lived in Nana's old house for a few months hoping that things would get better. It actually took a lot of convincing for Erica to agree to move there. No matter how hard we tried, and no matter how many hours I spent working late night jobs, it just never was enough. We didn't know the power of prayer or we just ignored it altogether. But prayer wasn't something that we did. My lack of acknowledgment of God didn't keep me from blaming Him when things weren't going just the way that I wanted them too. I always believed that He was doing all these things to make my life miserable because I didn't follow Him the way that I did when I was a child. He had removed football from my life twice, and over the next few years, He would remove even more because He was angry at me—or did He just love me so much that He would continue to allow hurtful things to happen in my life?

Momma always encouraged me to 'get back in church' or 'you need to take your family to church' and it got me angry at times. The times that I would actually go, I would always see someone that I had seen in a bar the night before or in recent weeks. One Sunday morning, I spotted a man that I had been in a drunken fight with just a couple of weeks before. I played that 'church is full of hypocrites' card on numerous occasions and that was my 'go-to' every time Momma would bring it up. I just wasn't interested in sitting through a sermon with a room full of people that were likely doing the same things that I was doing, and for some, I had proof that they were. I am sure that if I had actually listened to my mother's pleas and focused on Jesus in my marriage, it would have lasted.

The more I refused to add Christ in my marriage and my family, the worse everything became. I actually would say those little prayers that would include "God, if you do 'this', I'll do 'that', just take all of my troubles away". They were selfish prayers that remained unanswered and it angered me and dragged me further away from bringing Christianity into my home. I should have listened to my mother because it was her faith that kept her and Pop together all of those years through all the issues he had with alcoholism and Post-Traumatic Stress Disorder. My mom's unconditional love approach to her marriage was a direct reflection of her undying devotion to Jesus, but that wasn't enough to wake me up to the truths of the gospel and its effect on a marriage.

As time went on, our marriage continued to get worse. Bills were still going unpaid and I was still working as much as possible. I was doing well in school making the Dean's List for my first couple of semesters at West Alabama. School was the only thing that was going well. One morning when I was getting ready to leave for school and Erica and Logan were about to head out, there was a knock on the door. It was an unusual time of the morning to have a visitor or even a salesman to come soliciting their product. I was hesitant to open the door until I saw through a small opening in the blinds that a sheriff deputy car was in the driveway. I wasn't sure what to expect. Did Pop have a wreck? Had someone I had been in a fight with decide to press charges? Did something I do in my past finally catch up with me? Why was a deputy knocking on my door at 7 am?

I knew I had to answer the door if for no other reason, to know what he was doing there. I don't think I could get through the day if I didn't know what he was trying to accomplish even if it meant that he was there to arrest me for something. It wasn't quite as bad as being arrested, but it was the final blow in our decaying marriage. The deputy was there to serve us with papers notifying us that we had been sued by a financial services company that we had borrowed money from a year earlier. I borrowed some funds in order to invest in a company that I thought would be the answer to our financial problems. I never really worked the business the way that I should have and all of that borrowed money wasn't earned in order to pay back the loan.

Erica calmly informed me that she and Logan would not be coming back and she would be at her parents' house if I wanted to come get Logan until we worked out a visitation. Again, God was removing things from my life and it just didn't seem fair. My son was my motivation to succeed. He was the reason that I tried so hard to make ends meet while I went through school. He was the only reason that coming home in the evenings was an option. And now, I would be coming home to an empty house. I was upset that Erica and I couldn't make it work. We both contributed to the collapse of our marriage. We were both pretty stubborn in our arguments and there was seldom any common ground on issues that we differed on. Neither of us would admit any fault and apologize for anything. We had nothing in our marriage that would serve to keep it together.

Obviously absent from our marriage was a deep following of Jesus. Maybe our faith wouldn't have paid the bills and maybe our faith wouldn't have made us happy together, but faith in Christ does make things easier to deal with. In a Christ-centered marriage, we would at least have had hope and we would have valued our vows more deeply because they were cited in front of God and with Him in mind. We went about our marriage in conflict of what we were raised to value; love, respect and a love for Jesus and because of that, it failed.

For a long time, I didn't sleep a lot. I missed Logan so much that it caused me to really slip into a depression that I had never seen before. I had always known what worry felt like, but depression was a different animal. As I sat around the house all alone, I had way too much time to think about life and how bad it had become for me and how bad I had messed up so many things. I transferred to The University of Alabama so I wouldn't have to drive so much to class. Most mornings, I stayed in the bed. I had very little motivation to get me out of the bed and out of the door. When I left UWA, my grades were really admirable and I was proud of the accomplishments I was making in my education. My short stint at Alabama didn't go well due to my absences from class and I failed every class.

It didn't look very likely that I would ever finish my degree and that added to my depression. I consulted a psychiatrist at Alabama about what I was going through and was medicated for the many issues that my depression was causing. I was prescribed medication to help me sleep and some more for anxiety and depression. The drugs that I was given were highly addictive and they helped, until I started abusing them to fall asleep quicker and stay asleep longer. If I wasn't asleep, I was thinking and all that did was make things worse. I rarely left home for the next few months until football season rolled around again.

Football practice and all of the time I spent in preparation took a lot of my time and kept my mind off of things for a while. Matthew, our wide receivers coach moved in with me and that definitely helped me to ease the alone time that I had and slow down my abuse of pills. Matthew and I didn't exactly live like choir boys, but his presence at least got me out of the house on some evenings and I began to get motivated to start classes again. I transferred back to UWA and forgot all about the classes that I failed at Alabama. This time, I actually kept going to class and my grades were reflective of that. I was back on the Dean's List and heading towards graduation.

Although school had become a priority again and I was excelling, I still had a drug problem. After my prescriptions for anxiety and sleep ran out, I found ways to get my hands on pain killers—the kind that I had used for my surgeries. Since the first major surgery on my shoulder, I had two more by this time in my life and every time, the addiction got worse. I never took more pills than a doctor would recommend because as bad off as I was, I still had no desire to die. Although Logan wasn't with me every night like I had been accustomed to, I still wanted to be a great daddy and I knew how to cut off my addiction when he was around. However, I did learn that some of the pills that I had access to would work more intensely if I crushed them up as opposed to taking them whole.

Matthew and I would go to bars almost every night as long as Logan wasn't at my house. I started to meet a lot of new people and many of them were just as messed up as I was. These people were fun to be around until trouble would start at a bar and I would end up right in the middle of it. Violence would be reintroduced to my life and this time it was severe. It wasn't like when I lived on top of the hill at Knoll Circle and was fighting other kids. Now it was criminal and dangerous and it would take a tight grip on my life for the next few months. I struggled with the divorce for a very long time and the separation that it created between Logan and me. My time became flooded with drugs, alcohol and violence; but two thing s remained relatively the same—I was going to graduate and I was going to raise a great son.

Royce C. Brehm

Chapter Twenty-One

Fogged Vision and Bloody Hands

School was still going great as I continued to receive good marks in all of my classes. I was getting closer to becoming a junior in college. It was taking me so long to finish because I was never able to take a full load of classes because I still had to work and I wanted to coach. I was doing well as a coach and was getting the praise of many of the coaches that I was working with. I was having the time of my life. On days that Logan wasn't with me, I was out on the town trying to be the life of the party, crushing pills and drinking insane amounts of alcohol. I never mixed the two on the same night because again, I didn't want to die.

One night after I was in a huge bar fight involving a group of men from a neighboring county, I met a guy that was in that fight—on the same side that I was on. As we were talking on the tailgate of his truck after we escaped from the arrests that were made as a result of the fight, he asked what I was doing that Saturday night. He started telling me about paid fights that he and some friends were involved in and wanted to know if I wanted to go. He said on some nights depending on who showed up, there were large amounts of money that traded hands from betting on fights. I said "Sure, I'll come watch." He quickly informed me that he wasn't inviting me to watch—he wanted me to fight.

For a couple of years while I was still married, I trained in a boxing gym in Northport that has since developed a world heavyweight champion. I never competed but I trained with and sparred several professional fighters in preparation for their upcoming fights. I was pretty good at disciplined fighting but I was even better at fighting to create an unfair advantage. I wasn't sure if I would be any good at fighting in a circle of people with a lot of cash on the floor. I had never really been in a fight that was planned and without any anger or a reason that instigated the fight in the first place. But there was money on the line and fighting, so I was in!

That Saturday I met up with him and we headed to a boat landing on Lake Tuscaloosa. The parking lot was surrounded by water on one side and the other three sides were surrounded by steep cliffs that went straight up. Before we got out of the truck, he told me that if the police showed up to climb the cliff in the back and meet him by the road that would be about two hundred yards ahead. There were a lot of people there so I was just thinking that it would almost be impossible to get lost if I just followed all of the fleeing gamblers and fighters. As we walked up to the crowd of people, there was a circular opening in the middle where two huge grown men were slugging on each other. I was just trying to find a way to prepare myself to fight a person that I didn't know and find some kind of intensity to keep from getting hurt.

The guy that appeared to be in charge of the whole operation walked up and asked if I was 'the guy'. He handed me a slip of paper that had a name on it. It was dark where I was standing so the name was hard to read. I angled the slip of paper so I could see what it said. "Pinky vs The Guy". I was sure hoping that I was "The Guy" and that Pinky wasn't a sarcastic nickname for a three-hundred-pound killer. There was about forty-five minutes until I entered the circle so I tried to find out who Pinky was but before I could, he found me. He walked up and politely told me that I would be leaving on a stretcher. That turned on my intensity because as always, I was not going to be intimidated by anyone.

127

It was my turn and I got ready to walk to the middle of that circle of humans knowing that what I was doing was wrong. The guy that handed me that slip of paper was yelling out numbers and people were handing him stacks of money as he shoved it all in a pillow case. I didn't have a clue what that was all about but I knew that I was a huge underdog and the whole lot was betting against me. The guy that brought me there said that he put a 'stack' on me and we were eating steak when we were done. This whole thing sounded a bit like several movies that I have seen but this time, I was the star.

At this point in my life, I felt like all that I had in life was myself and Logan, but only part time. This whole scene made me feel even more isolated as I didn't know but one person that was there. I had been to that boat landing in the past to hang out with friends and drink beer but I never knew that this type of thing even existed in our city. I finally got to the center of the circle and a guy who appeared to be the referee checked my hands and my shorts I assume for weapons. He did the same for Pinky who was about four inches taller than I was and a lot heavier. I knew that I had better stay on my feet or I would be in trouble. There was no bell to start the action, but the referee asked us if we were ready and then he yelled "KILL!"

Pinky just stood in the same spot looking at me. When I didn't move, he turned to his entourage and loudly laughed and said this would be quick and easy. I was paralyzed and didn't know what to do. We stood there for about thirty seconds and then I looked in his eyes and grinned as he ran towards me. I stepped a little to my left and he stumbled and I threw the longest punch I have ever thrown and it landed right on the back of his head and he crumbled to the ground. I didn't know if I was supposed to continue the assault or wait for a count. Before I could figure it all out, the referee stood up from over Pinky's limp body and pointed at me as the winner.

As I was putting my shirt on, three police cars raced down the hill. I was handed an envelope and told to get up the cliff. It was a good thing that I wasn't fatigued because I would've never made it to the top. When I got to the top of the cliff with a firm grip on the envelope, I opened it to see a stack of money. As I walked to the road that I was informed to go to, I counted, $675. Not bad for ten seconds of work. When we met back up, I was informed that Pinky was known for ending fights quickly and that he had only lost once before and he avenged that loss by putting his opponent in the hospital with a fractured skull. That wasn't happening to me because I was done with that activity.

After that night, I knew I wasn't going back and I never saw the guy that took me again. Apparently as secretive as the events at the boat landing seemed to be, it was actually talked about in the bar scene a little more than I thought. I had a woman approach me one night offering me money to assault her ex boyfriend because he was harassing her. I agreed and followed through with the deal. After that, I was asked if I was interested in collecting on gambling debts. I declined that option; it seemed too much like the New York mafia movies. I was offered a job as a bail enforcement agent and a bouncer at a bar. But all I wanted to do was finish school and coach football. If I was going to fight anymore, it would be a spur of the moment deal during a night at the bars.

I eventually started boxing again as a way to throw some punches legally and maybe cure my craving for violence. One afternoon while I was punching a heavy bag, I felt a burning in the palm of my left hand. At the time, we were discussing me fighting some amateur fights in Birmingham and it looked like maybe I could make boxing into a little more than a hobby. This burning worried me. I was at the gym alone at the time and I couldn't get my glove off by myself so I drove to the hospital with it on. I ended up having carpal tunnel syndrome and some tendon damage. I didn't follow through with the plan of action by the doctor and did the same thing I did with my shoulder and ignored the pain and used my pill habit to make it bearable.

Royce C. Brehm

The nights were still lonely when Logan wasn't with me and a lot of nights, Matthew was gone to his girlfriend's house. My addiction was intensifying and that's really all I did at night. I would crush pills and play online poker until the early morning hours; but I wouldn't miss class. It was starting to get harder to function throughout the day. The 2005 football season had just ended and I didn't have a lot to occupy my time so my habits got worse. The late fall season and winter of 2005 was a terrible time for me. All of the things that I had put myself through over the last few years had brought me to a dark time and I had no one to help me out of it.

I had some good friends, but not many of them were there for me in a supportive way, but not many of them knew exactly what I was dealing with. I didn't talk about my addiction and I didn't talk about the other activities that I was taking part in like the boat landing fights and the minor, paid hits of harassing boyfriends. I didn't really reveal any of that until after my life changed from the events of early 2006. The nights that I laid in bed with a mind fogged with narcotics and alcohol were awful and I never knew that it would all change due to the biggest removal ever from my life.

Chapter Twenty-Two

Triumph from Tragedy

I was fortunate that Erica was always willing to let me see Logan. He always rode the bus to my parents' house after school and was there when I got home from class. I got to spend every evening with him before taking him home. Pop had finally retired from the Veterans Administration Hospital and spent most of his time with Logan or his Boy Scout Troop. Pop would always walk to the end of the road and wait for Logan to get off the bus. They were inseparable. Logan loved getting off the bus to his favorite person in the world and Pop felt the same way. Their relationship was unlike anything I had ever seen. It was special and Pop helped me in raising Logan to be such a great kid.

Throughout my life, Pop had severe drinking problems. I was always the sympathetic one because I knew the effects that the Vietnam War and his service there had on him. He rarely talked about any of it and I was always scared to ask. Reggie slipped up and asked one night exactly what Pop did in Vietnam. I looked at Reggie like I wanted to throw a knife at him. That question was off limits and I grew up knowing that. There were times in my childhood that Pop would have what they call flashbacks and at times it was scary. The most damaging part of his whole experience wasn't what happened during the war, but how they were treated when they returned.

Protesters angrily cussed at the soldiers as they returned from war and spat on them and threw objects at them. These heroes were treated like animals and it hurt my dad. He had given up a career in baseball to serve his country and he was treated like a criminal. I couldn't imagine the feeling that he and his fellow soldiers had as they thought they would return to a hero's welcome only to see the opposite. His job in the Army was tough. If you have seen any Vietnam War movies, he was the wild guy sitting behind the heavy machine gun in the open door of a helicopter flying over rice fields. He was shot down a time or two and suffered some permanent injuries to his elbow, wrist and leg.

Although Pop had to live his entire adult life with disabilities and mental torture, he still loved people. He loved his family and he loved Logan. He also loved Jesus even though at times, that fact could be questioned because he wasn't exactly living the life that God desires. He made attempts at seminary school and jail and prison ministry but neither materialized as the demons of his past always took over. In 2004, he began teaching Sunday School at nursing homes before he would attend church service. He gave his life fully to ministry and spreading the gospel message to the elderly. He also spent most of his free time cleaning up cemeteries with the Boy Scout troop that he helped lead.

He fell in love with camping. He camped in the summer heat and camped in the dead of the winter. Pop never got cold. I remember growing up, he would only wear a mechanics vest and short sleeve shirts, no matter how cold it was. Of course, as he got older, his tolerance to the elements changed and he bought a sleeping bag that would keep him warm. As he set out for his many camping trips, sometimes I wondered why he would sleep in a tent when it was below freezing. But being out in the woods with his friends and his troop was what he loved to do and it kept him from thinking about the horrors of the war and all that it took from him. Logan went on a few trips with him and he loved it. The scouts were a little older than Logan, but he also found a love for camping and it became a tradition for the two of us just before football season.

2005 was a great year for my parents when it came to their faith and their involvement in the church. Pop was fully involved in his ministry and it was improving his life. The whole time, momma was attempting to get me to come to church with Logan and of course, I made excuses. Eventually, momma stopped asking me and turned it all over to prayer. Momma and her friends stayed in prayer for me to come back to Christ. I was living such a horrible life at the time that I ignored all of it and just went about my business. I had all that I thought I needed in bottles.

After the 2005 season, I expanded my partying lifestyle and in December it all began to get worse. But soon, the final removal would take place and everything would change. Pop was admitted into the hospital because he was having minor seizures and bad headaches. It didn't seem to be very severe but he spent New Year's Eve in the hospital. I was hanging out with Jamey a lot at the time. Jamey was a great friend and being around him kept me from going overboard with my drug habit. We would just go out to bars and drink beer and go home. I never got into any fights when I was with Jamey.

On New Year's Eve, before we went out to celebrate the New Year, Jamey and I went to visit Pop at the hospital. He was doing well that night and we sat around and laughed as Pop told stories about me when I was a kid. Momma was there and before we left, she implored that we behave that night and be careful. We left the hospital and went to the same bar that we always went to in downtown Tuscaloosa. My plan was to not drink and after midnight, we would go to a place in Birmingham and hang out there until the early hours of the morning.

After we rang in the New Year, Jamey, I and two women jumped in my car and we went to the Five Points district of Birmingham to continue our evening of partying. Once we got there, it was still my intention to stay sober so we could get home the next morning. I decided to have one mixed whiskey drink and that would be it. I sipped that glass of whiskey and water and it was all I remembered about the evening. I have never known if there was something else slipped into that drink or if I just continued to drink so much that I became so intoxicated that my memory faded. My next memory of the night was brief as we ate breakfast at a restaurant down the street.

When I woke up, I realized that I was in the backseat of my car with the door opened and my legs hanging out onto the step rail. No one was in sight and my car was halfway in the street and half in the driveway of an unfamiliar house. I didn't know where I was or how I got there and it took quite a while to remember exactly who I was with the night before. I called Jamey's cell phone and asked where I was. I don't remember much of the conversation but I was at least able to know that I was back in Northport. I knew the town well so I just drove until I knew where I was. I got back to my house a slept for the rest of the day, New Year's Day, and into the next morning.

I never really found out much about what happened that night but I knew it was bad. I still don't know how we got back in town or where I was when I woke up. I spent January 2, 2006 still recovering from that night and watching football with Pop after he came home from the hospital. Logan was with me until he was due to return to school a few days later. We spent that day hanging out with Pop and he seemed to be doing just fine from his time in the hospital. It was the day of several of the year's biggest college football bowl games and we had a great time watching them.

Shara was planning her wedding which was coming up on January 28. We were all excited that she would be marrying Terry, who really was the only guy she had ever dated that seemed like he had some kind of a future. The stresses of wedding planning for a bride-to-be and the mother of the bride were definitely showing. When the women in my family are stressed, it is best to stay out of the way and let them plan in peace. Shara was home for the week as she and momma were planning a trip to Fayette, Alabama to look at the bridesmaid's dresses and to check on the work on her wedding dress. It was a fun time in the life of our family.

Two days later, on January 4, mom and Shara left to handle the business of the wedding and Logan and I were going to spend the day with Pop watching movies and waiting for the National Championship game that night between USC and Texas. After momma and Shara left, Pop wanted to take a nap so Logan and I went to town to grab some breakfast. We went to a barbeque restaurant that served some of the best breakfast around. We ate so much that we were ready for a nap too. When we got back to Pop's house, he was snoring like a grizzly bear. We were making fun of him and laughing so loudly that he woke up. Pop got out of bed and jumped in the shower and Logan and I settled in the living room to watch some movies.

When Pop got out of the shower, he said he was still tired and was going to lie back down and sleep a little more because he wanted to stay awake to watch the game that night. He quickly started snoring again; so loudly that we could hear him all way in the living room which was the entire length of the house. We turned the volume up on the TV as we watched *The Replacements,* a movie about back up football players that filled in as the professionals went on strike. It is one of my favorite movies. As it ended, we no longer heard the grizzly-like snoring from the back of the house.

Logan, who was almost nine-years-old then, got up to go check on Pop and was going to lay down with him until he woke up and I was planning to take a short nap on the couch. A few seconds passed and Logan came running back in the living room and yelled, "Daddy, Pop is purple and he has blood coming out of his mouth". His hysterical cries sprung me to my feet as I ran to Pop's bedside. He indeed was a shade of purple and had blood coming from his mouth and nose. I called 911 and picked Pop up and put him on the floor beside the bed bed so I would have a hard surface to do chest compressions because he was not breathing.

There was no way for me to know how long it had been since he stopped breathing. He had no pulse. I couldn't do any rescue breaths because he has a lot of blood in his mouth and I was concerned that it would just move that blood into his lungs and there would be no chance of saving him. As I was doing chest compressions, my mind went blank. This was the absolute worst moment of my life and I wish that I had a strong desire to pray in hard times because it would have helped at that moment. His pulse returned after I frantically pressed down on his broken sternum. It was a good sign as far as I knew.

Within minutes, the front door opened and in walked a familiar face. It was Keith, a sheriff's deputy that was also Logan's substitute bus driver. Logan frequently talked about Mr. Keith. He was one of Logan's favorite people. Keith was a year younger than I was and he was also in the State Trooper Academy in Selma at the same time that I was in the Corrections Academy. They were housed right next door to us and I would see him during drills, but we never spoke there or when we were in school together at County High. But I knew who he was and he entered the house at a perfect time because I was exhausted and didn't know what else I could do.

Matthew ran into Pop's house after realizing that something was wrong from our house down the hill. As I turned the rescue attempts over to Deputy Keith, I quickly started looking for Logan. I didn't even ask Matthew if he had run back to our house, I just ran out of the house to find him. Matthew yelled to me that Logan ran into Sam's house. Sam and Sue were our neighbors and their house was situated between mine and my parents' house. They were quite fond of Logan and they would regularly keep Logan after school when Pop and Momma were out. I went in to check on Logan and explained to them what was going on.

As the ambulance arrived, I went back up the hill to see what I could do to help and to check the severity of Pop's health at that moment. A paramedic told me that his pulse was still there and they had him breathing with a machine but there was no way to know how long he was without oxygen. His brain had obviously suffered some severe damage being without oxygen for who knows how long. They weren't really able to tell me what the future would be.

I called momma and told her that Pop was in an ambulance on his way to the hospital. I tried my best to stay as calm as I could in order to make certain that she or Shara was able to safely drive back to Northport. It was difficult to hold it together as I tried not to sugar-coat the situation but create a sense of urgency for them to get back to town. Uncle Ike, momma's brother sped to the house to pick me up to take me to the hospital. I didn't know which hospital they took him to—we have two in Tuscaloosa County, one in Tuscaloosa and one in Northport.

The hospital in Tuscaloosa was more capable of handling major traumatic cases so I figured we would start there. He wasn't there and we headed back to the hospital in Northport. The two hospitals were only about four miles apart but we made the trip back to Northport in less than two minutes. Uncle Ike spent a lot of time in law enforcement and was known to drive fast all of the time. I was glad that he was the one driving me to find my daddy. The rest of that afternoon is a blur in my memory. Logan stayed with Sam and Sue hen I left and momma and Shara eventually arrived at the hospital. Jackie and her husband, Todd got there that evening.

At the time Jackie arrived, Pop was still alive and we were really just in a waiting period to see how it went overnight. We watched the football game in the waiting room of the radiology department and then Jamey took me to Matthew's girlfriend's house for me to get some sleep. Logan went back to Erica's parent's house that night. As the adrenaline of the day wore off, I started getting really emotional at the thought of losing my dad. I grew angry and started blaming God as I had in the past so many times. I couldn't believe that after a life of alcoholism, pain and hurt that Pop had finally dedicated his life to Jesus, and now God was going to remove him from my life. I was completely done with this God that momma had begged me to seek. He had removed so many things from my life and this was the last time that I would allow it to happen and still allow my mom to talk to me about Him.

I crushed a couple of pills and went to sleep. The next day I went back to the hospital and nothing had changed. Pop's brain was almost completely dead. Momma said that the doctors started talking to her about organ donation and momma's reply was that she wanted to pray some more and hope for a miracle before taking Pop off of the life support that was keeping him alive. Their pastor, Ben, who was new to their church, came to the hospital chapel where we were all gathered. He prayed for a miracle to happen and for Pop to be healed. He spoke of an eternal healing and I kind of rolled my eyes in sarcasm. Through the rest of that day and in to the evening, people were coming by and praying for God's will to be done and for Pop to be healed on earth or healed eternally.

In my narcotic induced dizziness, I stayed calm, but I really didn't want to keep hearing about this eternal healing because in their eyes, that meant that I would lose my father. It wasn't fair that after the best year that he ever had in his faith, he was about to die. Eventually, late on January 5, momma started talking to me and my sisters about allowing the doctors to test Pop's organs in hopes that he still had something that functioned well enough to benefit someone else in need. I didn't want to talk about it at first. I didn't see any way that Pop had anything internally that would be in good enough shape to inject into someone else's body. And I refused to realize that he would never live through this.

I went into the trauma room where they had been keeping him for one last visit as I started to come to terms that I was losing him. There laid the strongest man I had ever known. He used to always make jokes about having nine lives like a cat on a television commercial because he had survived so many things. I guess this was his tenth life because the doctors said that there was nothing else that they could do. Pop had major auto accidents and lived. He endured the tortures of war, and lived. He had a heart episode when I was young, and lived. He almost lost his vision due to an accident at work, and lived. And now, he was losing his life because he had a seizure while sleeping and aspirated on vomit or blood, or both.

It appeared that Pop was such a strong human that it would take something drastic to take his life. It ended up being something simple and caused by the years of medication that he had to take simply to have a functional life. On January 6, 2006, Pop died and my whole world began to change at that moment. How would I handle an eight-year-old son who just lost his second grandfather in such a short time? Erica's real father died a year or two earlier from a short fight with brain cancer. And now, Logan was losing his best friend and the man who he ran down the steps of the bus to see every afternoon. How would Logan adjust without having Pop in his life?

I just couldn't be okay with the fact that Pop was taken from us at that time. It didn't seem right and it was completely unfair and couldn't have been timed any worse. He was living for his Lord and Savior. He was living the life that is talked about in Galatians Chapter Five. He was doing all the things that I thought would bring about happiness and good health. I had a terrible misconception of what it meant to be a Christian. I just thought that it made life better and all your troubles would go away. I had been in churches where everyone did one heck of a job of masking their problems in life so it just appeared to me that bad things didn't happen to good, Christian people.

I spent the next few nights popping pills and drinking. The carefulness that I had always taken in my addiction—not taking too much and not mixing pills and alcohol—was all dismissed and I did everything that I could do to numb the pain of losing my daddy. As people came to visit my mom at her house, I just sat there listening to them talk about Pop being healed and in a better place. My anger intensified the more I heard it. I didn't want to hear any of that. I don't remember the visitation or the funeral ceremony. To this day, I don't remember being there. I obviously didn't pay any attention to what was being said at the funeral because I knew that I wouldn't believe any of it. As one lady left the house the day of the funeral, momma told her that she would see her at church on Sunday. It would be just eight days after Pop passed away and she was going back to church.

That was exactly what I expected out of her. I knew she would just go on with life and I knew that what she believed about God would get her through it even though I didn't believe any of it. That night, I lay in bed and thought about how strong she was to get back to her routine so easily. I figured it was the least I could do to offer to go to church with her a few times so Pop's usual spot on the pew wouldn't be empty. I thought maybe it would make it easier on her if I was simply sitting there. On January 15, I went to church and just sat there inattentive waiting for it to end so I could go back home and eat lunch and watch football.

After that service, I walked with momma to get Logan from the Children's Church room. He was so excited about what they had learned that day and he started telling me all about it. I don't remember what the lesson was, but I do remember vividly how happy he was about telling me all about it. It really hit me hard that my son loved church and he loved Jesus and it was all because both sets of grandparents were doing for him all the things that I was not. He loved going to church and I wasn't the one that was taking him. It hurt me to think about.

The church always had a meal before Bible study on Wednesday evenings and momma asked if I wanted to go. Before I could say no, I remembered Logan's excitement the Sunday before and I agreed to go. I sat at a table with Momma and Logan and some of her friends. They were some really nice people and appeared to genuinely care that I was finally there with them. Logan couldn't eat fast enough in his excitement to go to his class and learn more about Jesus with his friends. It was just more for me to think about. His excitement had me curious. After he got up and ran to meet his teacher and his friends, a young lady that I knew walked up and invited me to Sunday School. She taught a singles class and there were a lot of people in the class that had been through similar things that I had been through.

I avoided showing up for Sunday school the following Sunday but I drove and met Momma and Logan for service. This time, I sat and listened to the sermon this time. That same man that prayed for my dad to be healed was preaching about eternal healing through salvation and what it meant for all who believed in Christ. I knew the belief that when you get to Heaven you would be with your loved ones forever, but the thought of that never crossed my mind until that moment. I heard what he was saying, but I felt like I had ruined my life so badly that I couldn't just make a decision to follow Christ. I didn't think that He had any use for a man like me. I had thoughts of cleaning up my actions so that maybe then, I could come to church and feel right about being there. I never sat and thought that I was actually there to have my actions cleaned up for me.

Over the next week, I thought a lot about seeing Pop again in Heaven, but I continued doing drugs and drinking every night. Every time I would think that I could be a follower of Jesus again and see Pop forever, I would talk myself out of it because of the terrible person that I was. I used the excuse that I needed to clean myself up first. This was the week of Shara and Terry's wedding and it caused me to become even angrier about the timing of Pop's death. It just added to the unfairness of the situation and made me think less of this eternal healing that I was so close to believing. My doubts would soon be erased at an incredibly uncommon time and my life would continue to change.

Chapter Twenty-Three

A Walk Down the Aisle to Eternity

The wedding planning was coming to an end and it was almost time for my baby sister to marry her fiancé. The whole week leading up to the wedding is a fog in my memory. I stayed as high as I could stay in order to deal with the fact that it was me, not Pop, that would be walking Shara down the aisle and giving her away. That has always been the dream of my sister, for Pop to give her away. Pop had an incredible sense of humor and I am certain that if it had been him that walked her, he would have done or said something that would have knocked the edge off and caused Shara to relax as she took her final steps as a single woman. It wasn't fair that that moment was different than she had imagined.

On January 28, just three weeks after losing Pop, I had to do the second most difficult thing I ever had to do—step in for my deceased dad in giving my sister away. I took enough pills to numb the nervousness and the anger that I felt for being thrust into this situation. As I arrived at the church, I could hardly walk. I didn't know how I would get through this and I was worried that Shara would break down and the whole ceremony would take a terrible turn. I love my sisters and no matter what state I was in in my life, I would do anything for them so I gathered enough energy to get myself together enough to do the duty that was passed on to me.

As we stood in the back of the church waiting to take our first steps, I began to relax and felt a sense of comfort come over me. The buzz of the pills lessened to the point that I could walk without stumbling but I was still intoxicated. I thought about what Pop might say in this moment and I drew a blank. I just knew that he had something planned that would burst Shara into laughter just before they came into the attendants' sight. I had to do that for her and I had to do it for myself too. If laughter didn't take over, there was no way that we would get to the end of that aisle without completely losing it. Our first stop at the end of the aisle would be at a candle in memory of Nana. The next stop would be one for Pop that sat right next to the very spot that he sat in for every church service he attended there.

There would be no way to light these candles with our family if the mood wasn't lightened in some way. As the music stopped, we knew that the wedding song would begin and we would be walking. She asked if I was ready and out of nowhere, I said something that had absolutely no meaning in relation to the situation. I didn't know where it came from or why I said it, but prior to the hardest laughter that I had seen out of the both of us in years, I looked in my baby sister's bloodshot eyes and exclaimed one of funniest lines in any Adam Sandler movie. It was my last words apart from Jesus so let's just say, it isn't appropriate for the context of what was about to happen in my life. It just came out and I am thankful that it did.

Instead of tears of sadness, we walked that aisle with tears of hysterical laughter. The shock in everyone's eyes was pretty humorous too. Everyone was prepared to see us crying in sadness and much to their surprise, it was the opposite. As we approached the first memory candle, Momma and Jackie couldn't figure out what we were laughing about. When they asked us, Shara simply told them that we would tell them later. After lighting candle in memory of Nana, we walked over to Pop's empty spot in the pew. The laughter quickly shifted to a sense of seriousness and Momma grabbed the lighter.

My thoughts and my emotions were quickly redirected to what Ben the pastor said about eternal healing and my intoxication from the pills suddenly disappeared. I actually felt God take over me and I felt a comfort like I had never felt. At that moment, I knew that He would be the One to clean me up and He welcomed me just the way that I was. All of my anger disappeared, all of my sorrow turned to hope and all of my sadness turned to anticipation. I was fully and eternally committed to Jesus Christ and I made that decision at a very uncommon time. I may have smiled throughout the entire ceremony eagerly waiting to tell someone that I was again in the arms of God.

The ceremony ended and I expected that my decision to follow Christ would soon fade away because it was such an emotional time when I made that decision. But the comfort that I felt never left me. The doubts I had that my addictions were lifted stayed far from my mind. I was confident in the promise of the gospel and it stayed with me. I couldn't wait to begin a new life free from addiction but I also knew that it wouldn't be easy and I couldn't do it without the help and support of God's people. I just knew that I needed to start attending that Sunday School class that I was invited to.

Chapter Twenty-Four

A New Creation

I was really taking my new life seriously. I woke up every day with a desire to follow Jesus—but it wasn't as easy as I thought. The temptations of my addictions were still very present but so was the strength that I drew from the Holy Spirit. I was fighting urges and I was winning, the majority of the time. I finally decided to attend Sunday School and try to get closer to people that were like me. The class was a singles class made up of people my age or older. We had all been married previously and were all dealing with similar issues so it was perfect for me at a time where I needed a diversion from the urge to drink or crush pills.

We all spent a lot of time together going out to eat or spending time studying scripture together. You would think that in a group of single adults we would all be trying to spark some kind of interest in each other, but that wasn't the case at all. It was a supportive group and everyone had concern for each other. I can't say that a few people in our group didn't end up in relationships, but the main concern was our faith and strengthening our walks with Christ. This group went a long way in keeping my focus on Jesus and I am forever grateful for their influence on me.

I did have one final time when my urges turned to action. I was a big NASCAR fan at the time. I loved going to Talladega Speedway twice a year to watch the fast cars and have a good time. Pop and I went a couple of times prior to him passing away. In April of 2006, I attended the races with a few friends that I had kept contact with from my past. These guys were not the worst friends that I ever had. They were the 'laid back' group of my acquaintances. I never got in any real trouble with them. The long day of watching races turned into my last fight with alcohol. I thought that I could turn off my temptations after having one drink. I should have known it wouldn't be that easy. One drink turned to two drinks and before I knew it, I was passed out in a Mexican restaurant in Hoover, Alabama that we stopped at on our way back home.

For the first time in my life, I felt regret for what I had done when it came to my addictions. It was painful! I called to talk to a man that was in my Sunday School class and told him what I had done and the subsequent shame that I felt as a result. He told me that this was the best news I could have told him! I was seriously confused on how this could possibly be good news. This man was always concerned about my wellbeing and now he was telling me that my drunken Saturday in Talladega was a good thing. He started telling me that God gives us His Holy Spirit to convict us when we go against His teaching. He said that this spirit is reserved for people who have actually accepted Christ and the fact that I was feeling conviction about what I had done was confirmation that I had made a real, permanent decision to live for Christ. It actually made sense to me and I was overwhelmed with excitement. On April 29, 2006 I got intoxicated for the very last time.

Hindsight Joy

There were times over the next few months that I had easy opportunities to fall back in to the former life that I lived. But the time I spent with my new set of friends helped steer me back in the right direction. My motivations were different. Life wasn't about me anymore; it was about serving my Savior and finishing school so Logan would have a better life. It was different making decisions based on God's will and not my own desires. I quickly realized that His plans for me were better than my plans for myself. My next goal was to get my degree and find my role in the ministry of the gospel.

Schoolwork became easier. I had been doing well in my classes although my conscious was sometimes littered with my addictions. It was difficult to attend to my studies with my flesh pulling me to do bad things. With my new found desire to serve Jesus, it really did get easier. From early 2006 until May 2009, I studied hard and my grades were stellar. After Pop passed away, I was fired from my coaching position at Bryant High School. The head coach wanted to have coaches that were on campus all the time so he did away with employing volunteers. I kind of saw this as a sign that I needed to step away from coaching until I completed my degree. It was a tough decision, but graduation was my next goal and I needed to focus on it.

At the time that Pop died, I was working at Collins Riverside Middle School in the alternative school working with students that had problems in a regular school environment. I saw a lot of the former me in those kids. I had compassion for them because I knew what they were dealing with. After the 2006 school year ended, I went in to that summer trying to finish as many college classes as I could. I didn't have any summer football duties and I would have plenty of time to go to class. I didn't have to work because as a teacher's aide, I was paid through the summer.

One June afternoon while Logan and I were eating lunch at a restaurant in Northport, I received a phone call from a number that I didn't have programmed in my phone. It was Mark Cochran who had just been named as the new football coach at Collins Riverside. He said that he wanted to meet with me about coordinating his defense for the upcoming season. I told him about my decision to step away from coaching for the time being but I was open to meeting with him about it. It didn't take long for that meeting to take place because he was actually in the same parking lot of the shopping center we were in eating lunch.

Logan and I drove over to the area that Mark was sitting and we met briefly about the offer. I knew right away that working for him would actually be a good idea at the time. He seemed to be a good influence and he assured me that coaching middle school football wouldn't have nearly the time strain that high school coaching had on me. I only took one night to make the decision to join Marks's staff. It turned out to be a great decision and I had a lot of fun coaching at that level. We started off a little solely trying to rebuild what was once the powerhouse middle school program in Tuscaloosa County. We played our first year with 18 players and stayed competitive in every game and even won four games. Our second year, we were three plays away from winning the championship and in year three, we won the whole thing.

I coached four seasons there with Mark and gained a lot of valuable experience while finishing school, but I wanted to coach high school football again! There was nothing like Friday nights in Alabama. I just had to get back on a Friday night sideline. Coach Clark was still at Prattville and he was becoming one of the most successful coaches in the history of Alabama high school football. My goal of coaching for him was looking bright but now wasn't a good time. I just couldn't leave town because that would minimize my time spent with Logan. I began to pray for God to reveal an opportunity for me to coach in high school again.

Chapter Twenty-Five

God, You Want Me to Do What??

During my first three years coaching at Riverside, I continued to do well in school. I was able to coach football and baseball there and have plenty of time to finish school. In May 2009, it all became reality! I scored nearly perfectly on the state teaching license exam and completed my teaching internship and was set for graduation. It was a day that I had waited on for a very long time. I was excited for myself, but I was overwhelmed with joy for my mom! She never gave up on me no matter how crazy my life became. She stayed in prayer for me to do something with my life and always had confidence that I would do something great. Her desires for me motivated me to get it all done. Seeing her teeming with pride on that day was one of the best things that I had ever witnessed. Having my family there in that overcrowded gym while I received my diploma was one of the best days of my life.

I spent that whole summer trying to find a teaching job. It was tough. Living in a large college city made it almost impossible to find work as a Physical Education teacher. Students would graduate from the University of

Alabama and they wouldn't leave! They would come here from different cities and they would stay. It was really aggravating that I couldn't get a job in my hometown because it was flooded with out of town graduates. I could have grown angry, but I believed in God's plan for me.

One afternoon as we were practicing for our first football game, my phone rang. The school year had already begun so I just figured that I wouldn't be teaching that year, at least until Christmas. The call was from the principal of a local elementary school telling me that their PE teacher had resigned and she wanted me to come interview for the position. Although I didn't think I was cut out for elementary school teaching, I was excited at the chance to interview. It was a tough interview in a room with six teachers and the administration. I really didn't think I stood any chance of impressing them enough to get an offer. I was surprised to get a phone call two days later to inform me that I had actually been offered the job and I obviously accepted.

That was a fun year. Funding cuts and the fact that my style of authority is more geared for older students made it my only year at Huntington Place Elementary. It was just another part of my life that God removed in order for me to get to where He needed me. Although life was great through all of this, I still had some struggles with loneliness. I didn't have Logan nearly enough to take the depression completely away from me. In September of 2006, I brought Eliza home. Eliza is my German shepherd and a huge reason that I am still living addiction free. If I didn't have Logan, I still had Eliza and she was enough.

It was now the summer of 2010 and I had only made futile attempts at dating a couple of times. God made it clear on both occasions that there was something else out there for me. I had been praying for God to send me to the right person for a while but that prayer was never at the top of my priorities. Eliza filled the void of being alone enough to make living alone bearable. But I knew that I still wanted to meet someone eventually. I felt like God wanted me to forget about finding a woman and let Him deal with that. So I just went about my life with His plan leading me.

My itch to coach on Friday nights was still dominating my thoughts. Darrin, the offensive coordinator from Bryant High was now at a smaller school south of Tuscaloosa. He had been the defensive coordinator at Hale County High School for a few years and had called me a few times to try and gauge my interest in coming to coach his linebackers. I never really thought much about it until the summer of 2010 when I found myself without a job again. Hale County didn't have any teaching jobs available, but I went and met with him about volunteering with the football team in the event that I couldn't find a job somewhere else.

The job search proved to be just as difficult as it was the first time and August arrived and I was still unemployed. I began searching for jobs outside of teaching that would allow me to coach in the afternoons. As it appeared that I was about to land the perfect job for my situation, I agreed to coach linebackers for Darrin. That perfect job never materialized so I found myself in the middle of a football season with no real paying job. I substituted on as many days as I could. Our head coach, Chris Hilliker let me work in his class as many days as he could just so I could make enough money to pay my rent. It was a tough fall to say the least. Our football season was successful though.

Before I went to coach at Hale County, I knew it was what God wanted me to do. I asked Him on several occasions why I was supposed to go there. It just seemed strange that God was directing me to a place to coach for free without a real teaching job. I felt the urge to disobey every time I asked 'why?' After I agreed to go, God started showing me things that were so incredible that I just laughed and said "Okay, Lord. I see why". I would soon see many reasons for me going to Hale County that would prove to be God's big plan for my life.

Chapter Twenty-Six

"Coach, My Momma Likes You"

My coaching experiences we youth league, Bryant High and Collins Riverside Middle school so I had seen many different types of student athletes. The things that I witnessed early on at Hale County were very different—almost comical at times. The first practice in the summer of 2010 was highly anticipated. I had not met all of the players as of yet so there were a few players that I met for the first time that day. One guy showed up in boots—on the practice field, not just showing up to change clothes. As players were walking onto the practice field, Darrin would fill me in on them. This guy is fast, this guy is mean, this guy has a screw loose, this guy is strong and then there was Tyler.

Tyler was a 14-year-old freshman about six feet tall and close to two hundred pounds. The description that I was given on Tyler was the lengthiest of all the descriptions that Darrin gave me. It was for good reason, too. He wasn't expected to be a starter that year but was expected to be a big contributor because he would be the first player off the bench in about five different positions. The one thing about the early description that I remember vividly was, "That is Tyler and if he can leave the girls alone, he will be the best player in the state." I couldn't even begin to figure out how that conclusion could be drawn on such a young player that had not spent a lot of time in a varsity football game. I guess only time would prove that notion, and it actually turned into perfect truth later on.

I quickly drew close to Tyler and a linebacker name Brett. The two of them seemed to be pretty close but Brett was year or two older than Tyler but only one grade above him. Brett was a very good football player and was the kid that I could count on to let me know the truth about things. If a team mate was dragging around and not giving his best effort, Brett would let me know. I always love to have a 'coach on the field' and Brett was exactly that for me early in my time at Hale County. About midway through our season, we were pretty successful. We had only one loss and were looking like we were in really good position to host the first round of the playoffs.

One afternoon at practice during a water break, an alert came across my phone about a tornado watch that was issued in the area. Moundville is the small town that Hale County is located in and it was about 17 miles from my apartment in Northport. Of course I was standing around Tyler and Brett at the time of the alert and I mentioned that we needed to have a flawless practice so I could get back to Northport before the storms hit. I wasn't aware at the time that the next thing that Tyler would say to me would change my life forever. "Coach, I have a single momma so you can stay at my house during the storms". This was an interesting offer from a kid that I barely knew. It was definitely funny especially when Brett followed it up with "And she is hot too Coach".

I just basically laughed it off and told him that I didn't think his mom would be fond of that idea. I didn't know who his mom was and I had never seen her. Practice ended in plenty of time for me to get home and hunker down for the storms that didn't even come. The next day, Tyler continued with his comical offers to meet his mom. One day he would inform me that his momma 'liked me' and the next day he would offer me her phone number. Each time I just shrugged it off and didn't give any of it much thought. After about two straight weeks of his shenanigans, I began to get curious about his mom.

Social media was now in its prime so finding out things about people was really simple. It was as easy as entering a name into a search bar and clicking a button. One evening when I got home from practice, I searched Tyler's momma. Facebook was obviously the preferred method at the time. I was hesitant, but I sent her the friend request that could possibly set me up for humiliation. Her name was Dana and she was just what Brett said she was—HOT! I looked at a lot of her pictures which were dominantly pictures of family and vacations. I was looking for pictures of her doing things that I couldn't approve of so I could forget that I even took to internet stalking of a woman that I didn't know. I found nothing.

To my surprise, Dana accepted my friend request that same evening but we didn't communicate immediately. But Tyler's advances on behalf of his momma continued. He would not give up trying to slip me her phone number. He insisted that she knew who I was and she liked me. He just kept on with his sixth grade methods of trying to set someone up on a date. I stuck to my previous responses and just laughed it off.

Our regular season ended and we did enough to finish second in our region and were able to host the first round of the playoffs. Our reward was hosting Clay County, a state football powerhouse who had to travel the first round because they had one bad night. Unfortunately, they didn't have a bad night against us. We lost badly! Our season ended at 8 wins and 3 losses. We spent an extended time in the locker room after the game consoling the players and reminding them that the season was a success and we had plenty to build on for the next year. It was solemn scene in that room. Players were crying, coaches were at a loss for words and it was just a sad time.

After Coach Hilliker talked a while and the players started to pack up their things, Tyler walked over to me and hugged me. I was thinking that this would be where the talented freshman would thank me for coaching him and talk about the offseason. Obviously, this wasn't what Tyler had in mind. As we embraced, he leaned in and said, "My momma is outside waiting for me. Come meet her". I explained it just wasn't a good time for that under these circumstances. As the room slowly emptied, I gather up my belongings and walked outside and saw Dana walking outside the fence heading to her car. We made immediate eye contact and I knew that I may have made a mistake in not accepting her phone number from her son. But there was always Facebook, the ultimate pick up line portal.

I sat in my car for a few minutes trying to figure out some kind of slick way of beginning communication with her. What should I say? What kind of line could I send that would give me some wiggle room just in case she shot me down and wasn't even remotely interested? It was so obvious. I had just finished a season coaching her son who just happened to have loads of talent and unlimited potential. That was open door! She was single mother raising a son that needed as much correction as possible! I opened the messaging portal of Facebook and started typing my subtle offer of helping her son in life and hoping it would lead to conversations about other things.

I started off by telling her that it was a joy coaching her son—the obvious beginning. I offered to drive down to Moundville at any time if she needed me to come beat some sense into him. I never intended to actually do any of the stuff that I offered. I was just looking for a something that would indicate that she was interested in meeting me. I nervously hit the send button and waited. I spent the whole night refreshing the app hoping that a favorable response had been sent. Morning came and I was still waiting.

I drove to a local high school the next morning to watch Moundville's youth league play for the championship. I had watched a few of their games and they had some really talented players. As I was walking in the gate, my phone alerted me that I had an unread text message. It was from Dana! I gave her my cell phone number in my message hoping that she would use it. In my initial message, I told her that I would be trying to find permanent employment since the season was over. I guess that was her open door to message me back. We texted back and forth during the entire youth football game mainly about what kind of work that I was looking for and finally it led to normal text conversations.

She appeared to care a lot about trying to help me find a job. It was the first indication that she was an incredible woman. We texted each other that whole day and then late into the night. It was obvious to me that I just had to meet this woman. In one day of texting I had a great feeling about her and I knew I wanted to know more. She gave me that teenage boy throat lump and that crazy feeling in my stomach from the first text. Finally, we made arrangements to meet and I was pretty excited about it. The only question I asked my self was why I didn't take Tyler up on his offer to get her phone number weeks before.

Chapter Twenty-Seven

The Confirmation

Dana and I had our first meeting at her house. Tyler was there at the beginning of the night and Dana's daughter, Kelsie too. Kelsie was an eight-year-old cutie. She was a lively little girl that wasn't shy about being around someone new. She quickly informed me that I would be playing against her in some board game and the right to refuse was not available. It wasn't a request but a demand. It wasn't a game that I really could get into but it beat sitting on the couch awkwardly while Dana packed the bags for the kids to go visit their dad. After we finished one round of the board game I walked over and sat down on the couch and Kelsie quickly followed.

As soon as I looked up at what was on the television, Kelsie climbed up in my lap as if she had known me for years. I didn't really know what to make of her doing this but she didn't leave any doubt for long. She looked at me smiling with her huge gaps between every tooth and gave me a look of guilt. About the time I smiled back, she broke wind right on my leg. It wasn't what you would expect from a little cute eight-year-old. I had no idea how to handle this situation so I did what I would regularly do and I busted into laughter and told her that I would repay her soon. I wondered if this was her way to run me off because she didn't like the idea of some strange man being around her mother. This was the same method that I used with Jackie when she brought boys to the house while we were growing up so it made sense.

Tyler and Kelsie were there with us while they ate their supper and waited to be picked up. When their ride arrived I was ready to ask Dana if she thought Kelsie had a ploy to get rid of me. Kelsie got up from the table, grabbed her bag and walked over to me and gave me a big hug and asked if I would be there when she got home on Monday. I was thrilled!! There was no way that she would hug me and ask that question if she wanted me gone. That little girl made a great first impression on me and I couldn't wait to see her again. The rest of the evening, Dana and I watched Mixed Martial Arts on TV because I was a huge fan and watched her favorite movie afterwards.

As the evening ended she walked me out and I had that crazy teenage feeling that one day really soon I would love this woman. Trying to remember things during our first week of seeing each other is difficult. Two events happened to me as I was leaving their house that are really worth mentioning; I just don't remember if they happened the first, second or fifth time I went to see them. One night, I got in my little car that was affectionately known as "The Biscuit" due to its tiny size and I was completely out of gas. I had to reluctantly walk back up and ring Dana's doorbell to inform her that I wasn't able to leave. It was completely embarrassing. She thought it was hilarious and so did Tyler. I just saw it as her opportunity to do away with our new relationship. Dana is really big on being responsible and I was showing her that I was really lacking in that area.

On another occasion I walked to The Biscuit to find a flat tire. Again, I had to ring her doorbell and inform her that I wasn't able to leave. She drove me to the local store to buy a can of flat tire sealant. This wasn't my first time to use a can of this miracle patchwork. The whole process is easy—you twist the valve onto the tire stem and push a button—and I was an experienced professional at it. But somehow this time was different and I was just adding to her list of excuses that she could have used to make sure that I never came back. Apparently I didn't have the valve firmly on the tire stem and when I pressed the button the tire sealant shot me all over my face. When that liquid dries it turns to a leathery layer and it dries quickly!

How could I continue to embarrass myself that many times in such a short period of time and this fantastic woman continue to have me back to her house? Another shameful walk back to her door to tell her that I couldn't leave. This time my eye was pasted shut with tire sealant and burning like a thousand fires. My skin was red and my pride was once again shattered. But instead of Dana feeling concerned for me she laughed hysterically as I scrubbed the sealant off of my face. With my sense of humor, I was relieved at her response. I guess in a way it was really funny and I could see that fact through the burning of my skin and the temporary blindness that I was experiencing.

Our time together was always fun. Our relationship quickly grew into something great and while she was gone to the beach to shop over Thanksgiving weekend I found myself missing her badly. One night while she was gone I texted her and told that I couldn't wait for her to get back home. I was ecstatic when she informed me that she missed me too. In such a short time, I grew so fond of Dana and her kids and every moment with them was great. That Christmas, I was introduced to her family. Dana comes from a large family. This family is really close and they find reasons to meet together often. Birthdays—for every single one of them—is always cause to meet and eat together.

Spending a first Christmas with new people can sometimes be intimidating but they made me feel right at home and gave me a sense of belonging. Dana's parents are loved by the entire community. Every kid in town knows them simply as Mawmaw and Pawpaw. Her brother, Tony became the Mayor of Moundville during my second year coaching at Hale County and his wife Brandi serves on the county school board. They have three kids; Charlie Mak, Bubba and Bo. Logan and I felt like we had been a part of this family for years and we are blessed to be around these amazing people.

Chapter Twenty-Eight

The Unexpected Call

God has a way of amazing me. I never know what He will come up with next. In 2011 I was fully on board with His plans for me and I was diligently praying to be shown what was next. I had spent the last four years teaching middle school Sunday school at Five Points and I enjoyed being able to do that. I never felt like God would call me into ministry aside from what He already had me doing. One day at football practice our quarterback, Grant Stevens was talking about his youth group not having a youth pastor. His father Scott was the pastor at Moundville Baptist Church, the largest church in town.

I didn't think much about the conversation that Grant was having with team mates. I never thought that I would ever be called to youth ministry. At this time, I had never prayed out loud when anyone could actually hear me. Organizing events and discipleship curriculum wasn't things that I was very skilled at and I had no practice. I was still unemployed and just substituting for teachers at the high school but applying at the church never crossed my mind—until late one night while I was reading the story of Moses who had a terrible speech problem. I prayed for God to give me a reason to look into the open ministry position. The very next day, Grant handed me a piece of paper with his dad's email address and said that I should ask about meeting with him.

After a few days of prayer, I emailed Scott and we began to meet on occasion discussing the possibilities of me being called to this ministry. Just like it appears in almost every ministry position that I have known about, this was a lengthy process. Weeks would pass when nothing was being discussed and the prospects of this happening were diminishing. Scott emailed me one afternoon and asked me to come back to meet with him. He had met with the personnel committee and they wanted to meet me. My prayers quickly turned to asking God to give me the strength to answer His call to ministry if it actually materialized. I didn't think that I could do it and I was terrified at the thought of failing.

I had never been so nervous going into a meeting. Interviewing for jobs had become a regular routine for me and I never had a nervous moment in those settings. But what I walked into that afternoon was intimidating. I was a single father who had been divorced and I didn't think that this committee would overlook those details and have faith in me to serve. The questions were tough and the looks that I was getting were sometimes scary. I was truthful in everything and shared my salvation story with them and the meeting ended with something that I wasn't expecting at all. One committee member turned to Scott and asked him how quickly they could get this process done and get me there.

After the hard hitting questions and the honest answers that I had to give I didn't think there was any way that they would show any favoritism toward the idea of having me as their youth pastor. I met with Scott the next day and he described to me the steps that were left to take place. The church voted unanimously to call me as their new youth pastor and I accepted. I was absolutely scared to death. The people at Moundville Baptist were so welcoming and helpful so the transition was relatively simple. When I was informed of what I would be doing on my first day on the job I was floored! I would be going to the beach with twenty-something kids. Nice way of throwing a new minister into the deep end!

After about six months of meetings and prayer I headed south with all of those kids on what was their last day of school for that year.

Chapter Twenty-Nine

And I could Not Ask for More

Serving in youth ministry is a lot of fun. Sure, it has its ups and downs but the rewards are incredible. When I witness a student accept Jesus as their Lord and Savior, I get a deep feeling of overwhelming satisfaction. Over the next few months, the group grew into large numbers. We had a worship service every Wednesday night and we regularly had close to one hundred kids in attendance. God was doing incredible things in that place and I was just the lucky man that was allowed to be a part of it.

As the group grew in numbers, Dana began to take a big role in the ministry. I have no trouble in admitting that I am a terrible planner and not very good at being organized, but Dana is. When you think of great teams, you think of different people who excel at things that other team members fail at. That is the exact situation with Dana and me. There is no chance of getting her to speak in front of big crowds; but I love doing that. There is no way that I could plan an effective retreat and have all the minor details in place; but Dana can. So we make a great team.

I quickly learned that our teamwork also was critical in life as well as the ministry that God was building through us. I had never been good at money matters and my credit rating showed that fact. Dana is ALWAYS on top of finances. In all of my single man years I had never let anyone but Logan come in my apartment-it was always a mess. I just never saw the need in being clean if I was always by myself. I rarely did laundry and would regularly go to work with a scented drier sheet in my pocket to mask any smell that may be coming from my clothes. That is just the life I lived. Dana on the other hand was a cleaning machine-a laundry professional. It was quickly obvious that she was great at EVERYTHING I was bad at neglecting.

When pieces fit so well together in a puzzle, you get a beautiful picture. Sometimes that picture is of God's creation, an animal, a classic car or children's book characters. If you were able to look at my life as a puzzle you would see gaps that I had been praying to fill. Dana fills all of those gaps. How could possibly ignore that any longer. We had been together for over ten months and watching the pieces fit together gave me so much faith in the reasons that God sent me to her. Dana was so good to Logan and me. One of the most critical roles of a believer is to hold others accountable and boy was Dana great at doing that for us.

Thoughts of proposing to her never left my mind from early summer of 2011 until the fall when I knew that she was who God intended for me to marry. If I knew it to be true, why would I even consider waiting any longer? I had this great plan to propose to her at one of our Wednesday night services but I hadn't asked her dad for her hand yet. The day came and the ring was purchased and I still was trying to find the courage to ask Pawpaw to marry his daughter. I had to be at the church that day by 5:00 p.m. and I knew that time was running out as my chest started pounding and nervousness took over. What would I do if he said 'no'?

It was midafternoon and I drove to Dana's parents' house not even knowing if Pawpaw was there. As I pulled into the driveway I spotted him getting out of his truck and he looked directly at me as I drove down the long driveway—there was NO turning back. I eased out of my car and walked up to the intimidating man and nervously asked him the pressing question. I think the actual wording was "Can I have your permission to ask Dana to marry me?" He quickly agreed and smiled but with a few conditions—treat her like she deserves and don't fail. Those conditions were simple enough. It was scripturally based.

I snuck our parents into the balcony so that Dana wouldn't see them. As the service began, I had Dana, Tyler, Logan and Kelsie sit on the front row so they could see the video that I had prepared with pictures of Dana, the kids and me. As the video rolled, a friend of mine sang the song 'I Could Not Ask for More'. As the song concluded, I got on one knee in front of her and asked her to be my wife. After she gave the only favorable answer possible—yes—our parents came down and we took hugs and handshakes of congratulations for a few minutes before we began the worship time. Imagine asking the biggest question of your life just before walking on stage to preach. It was a nervous hour, but it was an awesome night.

It was October and we quickly went to work planning the big Day. Tony and Brandi were in the process of building a large beautiful home in Moundville and that is where Dana wanted to tie the knot. We frantically put the finishing touches on the yard at the house so it would be ready just in time for the wedding. We set the date for May 26, 2012. It was brutally hot that day but it didn't put any sort of damper on the events. The wedding was beautiful and the reception was a lot of fun but I couldn't wait to leave and head off for our honeymoon to the Dominican Republic. There are days that I have second-guessed the things that I have done but this day is not one of those. God sent me the rest of the puzzle and I am the most blessed man in the world for it.

Chapter Thirty

Glory to God

If my life was made into a movie, there would be many moments that may bring the audience to tears. I sure haven't lived the cleanest of lives. I have been fortunate throughout all of my mistakes to have plenty of people that loved me and diligently prayed for me although I ignored it for a long time. When I start thinking about all the things that God has blessed me with in the last decade, I can't help but wonder how I deserve any of it. Back in 2006 when I surrendered to Christ, the first book of the Bible that I read was James because it was short. As I look back on that questionable beginning I see why God led me to that text.

"Consider it a great joy, my brothers, whenever you experience various trials". THAT was the second verse that I read as a new believer. I was a man that question God on a regular basis and I always wondered why he allowed things to continue to happen to me. When I read this verse, it hit me like a ton of fallen bricks. I asked myself, 'How can I possibly consider the loss of my father and so many other things that were important to me great joy?' What good could possibly come from loss, violence and addiction? I felt like this particular verse was only talking to believers who face trials but it didn't take long to figure out that my past experiences would one day be used to glorify the God that saved me from death.

Today I am still in the same youth ministry at Moundville Baptist and seeing God work all the time. I am still coaching and teaching at Hale County High School and praying for God to use me there to show Christ in a public school. I am now the head softball coach and we have won four of the last five state championships while I was an assistant and I pray that my teams will see our success as a platform to share the gospel. I want to see joy in successes just as I have found in my trials. Dana and I continue to take on adventures with two things in mind; impact the lives of kids with big dreams and share Jesus!

Tyler has become a hard working young man and is excelling in a career in architectural building. Logan is in the beginning stages as a Police Officer in Birmingham and though it makes me nervous, I know his salvation is secure and he uses his job as a gospel sharing platform. Kelsie is in the last two years of high school and is my catcher. She will move on to play at my alma mater, the University of West Alabama. Our kids have all grown into great young people. They have had their fair share of problems, but none have let their lives spiral out of control the way that I did. I look forward to seeing how God uses those three incredible people in their futures.

My life has been interesting to say the least. If I could go back and change anything, I wouldn't even consider it. This isn't because I wouldn't have wanted to give up the terrible things I had been doing, it is because it was all part of the story that God was writing for me. I can't change my past, but what I can do is try my best to help people see that they shouldn't wait for a tragedy to see Jesus for who He is! Naturally I would have loved to have given up on myself and accepted Jesus prior to all the mistakes that I made but I am right where God wants me because of it.

How can I look back and consider my tragedies as great joy? I am not sure how long I would have lived if God hadn't changed me through those circumstances. I was surely on a direct path to destruction. The death of my dad woke me up to the death of my Savior and I easily find joy in that. How do I find joy in losing my ability to play football? This situation began a desire to coach and with that desire, God has given me a battlefield in which to do His work. How do I find joy in a broken marriage? Erica and I are both happy now. We teamed up to raise an incredible son and I am not so sure he would have the same impact on people if he had to grow up in the kind of environment that we put him in. We are all better for our past trials.

My new life in Christ is definitely not free from trials. I still struggle with things, but who doesn't? The trials I face today serve to strengthen my faith just like the remainder of the James chapter 1 tells me they should. So how does James 1:2 apply to my trials as a nonbeliever? I look back and see how my story was written. I look back and see how everything happened at the exact time that it should have. I can see great joy in the disaster that God saved me from. I am a walking example of God cleaning up a man's mess and using him for His glory. I tried to change many times, but it took Jesus to do it right. In hindsight, I do find great joy in the removal of things from my life and the redemption that came from them.

I plan to continue in the work that God has me doing. I have terrible days that
make me want to give up and walk away from it. But those days are joyous for me because I know that Satan is trying his best to derail me. If it remained easy for me, Satan wouldn't have to worry about what it is that I am doing. If I am not giving the devil a hard time, I am doing it all wrong.

My message is clear—God wants you where you are. Don't try to change yourself because it just doesn't work. I am proof to that. Having Jesus in trying times is way better than seeking something else to give you peace. Substances are not the answer and the world brings nothing of everlasting satisfaction. Seek Christ and feel the pure joy of salvation and a Heavenly Father that knows you by name.

52621044R00105

Made in the USA
Columbia, SC
10 March 2019